THE EXPECTATIONS
OF MORALITY

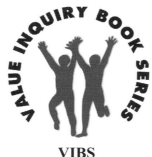

VIBS

Volume 158

Robert Ginsberg
Founding Editor

Peter A. Redpath
Executive Editor

Associate Editors

THE EXPECTATIONS
OF MORALITY

Gregory F. Mellema

Amsterdam - New York, NY 2004

Cover Design: Studio Pollmann

The paper on which this book is printed meets the requirements of "ISO 9706:1994, Information and documentation - Paper for documents - Requirements for permanence".

ISBN: 90-420-1742-2

To Jenna,
My Adorable Daughter

CONTENTS

EDITORIAL FOREWORD

Nicholas Wolterstorff

For most of the twentieth century, ethical theorists primarily focused their attention on the ethic of action; and within the ethic of action, the good and the obligatory were the basic categories of analysis. Theorists understood the morally obligatory as a particular species of the morally good; and a principle challenge they saw facing them was to explain what more must we must add to an action good for us to do to make it something obligatory to do: what more must we add to make an action something such that, if we fail to do it, we are morally guilty?

Some thirty-five years or so ago, the ethic of the agent gained the attention of theorists, in the form of virtue theory. This event immeasurably enriched ethical theory. In one way or another, some theorists tried to reduce the ethic of action to virtue ethics; more customarily, however, they saw the ethic of action and the ethic of agent as two independent, though interacting, dimensions of moral evaluation.

Gregory Mellema's *The Expectations of Morality* represents a strikingly innovative intervention into this discussion. The focus of Mellema's work is, once again, on the ethic of action; but Mellema shows that, if our theories are to catch the richness of moral evaluations of action, we need to identify and analyze more than the category of morally obligatory as a subcategory within the morally good. Admittedly theorists had always recognized a few additional categories—for example, the category of the superogatory. A superogatory action is one that is good to do without being obligatory to do, and whose performance, in addition, makes the agent praiseworthy. Mellema strikes off in a new direction altogether.

In our everyday lives we all form expectations about what our fellow human beings will do, and we act accordingly; I mean to say, we all form beliefs as to what our fellow human beings are likely to do. But quite a different concept of expectation exists with which we also operate, distinct from this predictive concept. Usually when we tell people what we expect of them, we are not informing them of what we predict they will do—we may even believe that they will not do it—but informing them of what they should do, on pain of being blameworthy. Some things are expected of us as college or university students, and as college or university professors; as medical patients, and physicians; when we are near a door and see someone struggling to open it, and when we see a child wandering about lost in a shopping mall. In all such cases, our failure to do what is expected of us reflects poorly on us; we become appropriate subjects of disapproval, blame. The concept of expectation employed in all these cases is normative (evaluative).

We are morally obligated to perform some actions we are normatively expected to perform; failure to perform the actions makes us blameworthy in that specific way which consists of being morally guilty. But Mellema argues, with great cogency, that this is not the case for all normative expectations; some of what is normatively expected of us is not something whose non-performance would make us morally guilty. Blameworthy, yes; but not guilty. Thereby he opens our eyes to a whole rich category of moral evaluations that has eluded our theorists, even though, in the everyday, we all work with the category of the normatively expected in our lives. To pay no attention, in our theories, to any other subcategory within the good than that of the obligatory (and the superogatory) is to treat the realm of the moral as far more rigorous and forbidding, far less rich in its differentiations, than it actually is.

In Chapter Three of his discussion, Mellema argues that, while no philosopher has thus far offered a sustained analysis of this concept of the normatively expected, some philosophers have, at least in passing, identified it. I am dubious about this second point. All of the passages he cites strike me as using the concept without identifying it, as we all do in our lives in the everyday, or as identifying and using that other concept of predictive expectation. Thus I think Mellema's discussion is more innovative that he appears to think. No sustained analysis of the concept has occurred. And I am not convinced that any previous philosopher has even so much as identified the concept. At least, none in the Western tradition. Mellema cites passages from Islamic thinkers in which, so I think, the concept is identified — or, if not this precise concept, something quite close to it.

I must not give the impression that Mellema spends the bulk of his tme identifying this concept of normative expectation. Of course, that was necessary; given the tradition, we all enter the discussion inclined to think that normative expectation is just moral obligation. But Mellema goes well beyond identification to give us an account of normative expectation. He shows what such expectation comes to, how the concept relates to other categories of moral evaluation, how what is normatively expected of us relates to our knowledge of what is normatively expected of us, and so forth.

I predict that some time will have to pass for those who work, or read around, in moral theory, fully to absorb Mellema's contribution. Many attempts will occur to argue that the old familiar categories of moral obligation, supererogation, suberogation, and the like, are quite sufficient to deal with the phenomena that Mellema indicates. I should add one prediction: eventually others will see Mellema's discussion as having shattered the old rigidities and made us see that the ethic of action is far richer, far less stereotyped, than we have been taught to think. This is one of those books that opens up a whole new, and intriguing, vista.

Nicholas Wolterstorff
Noah Porter Professor
Department of Philosophy
Yale University

ACKNOWLEDGMENTS

Portions of Chapter Eight are derived from my essay, "Symbolic Value, Virtue Ethics, and the Morality of Groups," which appeared in *Philosophy Today*, 43 (1999), pp. 302–308. I wish to thank the editor of this journal for permission to include this material.

I wish to thank members of the Calvin College Philosophy Department, including former members C. Stephen Evans, John Hare, and Lambert Zuidervaart for a great deal of helpful criticism. I have also received valuable responses to earlier drafts from Robert Audi and Nicholas Wolterstorff.

One

INTRODUCTION

One afternoon you are in a store and notice a sudden downpour of rain as you finish paying for your purchases. You decide to wait until the rain subsides before leaving the store and walking to the parking lot. Suddenly a woman with her arms full of packages is at the door struggling to enter, but she cannot manage to open the door. You are standing two feet from the door and can easily open it for her. You proceed to open the door, she enters the store, and thanks you for assisting her.

In this scenario I contend that opening the door for the woman is an act that you are morally expected to perform. It is an example of what I will call moral expectation. You are in a position to help her out, doing so requires almost no effort on your part, and no reason exists why you might refrain from doing so. Opening the door is something that anyone present could correctly expect you to do, and such an expectation is an expectation of a moral nature. You can be morally expected to open the door.

For suppose that you decline to open the door. Suppose you adopt the position that the woman has no right to your opening the door for her, you being a perfect stranger, and that you are perfectly within your rights to stand by and watch her struggle. I believe that this attitude would strike most people as callous or even mean-spirited. Perhaps someone could make the case that it is your right to stand there and do nothing, and perhaps someone could make the case that the woman has no right to your opening the door for her. But even if this were so, you could not deduce that your inaction is not worthy of criticism on moral grounds. Regardless of the rights each participant happens to have, inaction in this scenario is simply wrong.

The concept of moral expectation is a concept with which all of us are well acquainted. Already as children we learn that certain courses of action are expected of us. We are expected to perform certain actions, and we are expected to refrain from other actions. Furthermore, we learn that the failure to carry out these expectations can result in consequences and we come to understand that, at least some of the time, these consequences are deserved. Something is wrong with the failure to do what we are expected to do, and, more specifically, something is morally wrong with the failure to do what we are morally expected to do.

A central theme of this book is that moral expectation should not be confused with moral obligation. To say that a person is morally expected to perform an action is not necessarily to say that the person has a moral obligation or a moral duty to perform the action (I will not draw any distinction between moral duties or obligations), and this is true regardless of whether the duty in question is perfect or imperfect. A person can be morally expected to do some things which he or she is not morally obligated to do.

This, in fact, is true of the example just described. Although opening the door for the woman is something that you are morally expected to do, to say that you have a moral duty or obligation to open the door is doubtful. Moral duties and obligations comprise the demands of morality, and to say that morality demands of you that you open the door is excessive. After all, the woman's expression of thanks appears appropriate to the situation, and this is at least a slight indication that you were not just doing what morality demanded of you. Accordingly, since the violation of moral obligation can be described as that which is morally forbidden, judging that the failure to open the door is morally forbidden is likewise excessive. The failure to open the door is worthy of moral blame, but it does not warrant being described as morally forbidden.

The example, then, appears to be a case of moral expectation but not a case of moral obligation. The reasoning presented in the previous paragraph is hardly a proof that you have no moral obligation to open the door. And those who are skeptical that moral expectation can exist apart from moral obligation will hardly be persuaded by this line of reasoning. Nevertheless, we can plausibly judge that this is a case which falls short of moral obligation. More importantly, the general thesis that moral expectation and moral obligation do not always coincide is a thesis which is defensible, and in subsequent portions of this discussion I will urge that the denial of this thesis is counter-intuitive.

The thesis that moral obligation entails moral expectation is worth noting. Whenever a person has a moral obligation to perform an action, the person can be morally expected to perform the action. A moral agent can always be expected to carry out his or her moral obligations, and hence a moral obligation binding upon a person which the person cannot rightly be expected to carry out is impossible. If morality demands that a person perform a particular action, the person can surely be morally expected to perform it. Thus, while I have maintained that moral expectation does not entail moral obligation, the reverse entailment holds true.

If the positions I have stated about the relationship between moral obligation and moral expectation are true, then instances of moral obligation form a subset of the class of instances of moral expectation. All instances of moral obligation are instances of moral expectation, but not all instances of moral expectation are instances of moral obligation. The category of moral expectation is wider than that of moral obligation. It encompasses certain actions, such as the example discussed previously, which fall outside the scope of moral obligation. But no examples of moral obligation can be found which fall outside the scope of moral expectation.

If the categories of moral obligation and moral expectation were precisely the same, undertaking an investigation of the latter would be of little point. But if the category of moral expectation is wider than that of moral obligation, the situation is different. If actions which people are expected but not obligated to perform are possible, we can reasonably regard this class of actions as worthy of investigation. This is especially the case given the frequency with which moral expectation is referred to in ordinary discourse. The concept of moral expectation is familiar in ordinary discourse, and it is spoken of frequently in discussions of morality in the philosophical literature.

At the same time the concept of moral expectation has not been the object of investigation or analysis in its own right. People have a relatively clear idea of what is meant when they are told that they are expected to do something, and people frequently refer to moral expectation both in ordinary discourse and in philosophical discussions of moral issues. But no one has attempted to provide a systematic investigation or precise account of the concept of moral expectation.

In this study I will assume that moral expectation exists, and I will attempt to explain this concept in a manner which makes reasonably clear sense of how it is spoken of in ordinary discourse. The account I provide is not designed to correct what I consider to be mistaken beliefs about moral expectation by those who speak about it. The account I provide, rather, is designed to provide clarification of its use in informal conversation. And an underlying assumptions in this study is that such clarification can lead to a better understanding of morality. On a general level, it can help all of us to better understand a dimension of the moral life that has received surprisingly little attention in the literature. And on the level of attempting to live the moral life, it can give us more depth of insight into the moral evaluation of our own actions.

Not all instances of the words "expect," "expected," and "expectation" are relevant to the moral issues under consideration. Suppose someone has an expectation that Mr. Smith will be reading the newspaper at a particular time. This type of expectation functions as a mere prediction, and no effort need be made to express anything resembling a moral judgment. When the expectation in question is nothing more than a prediction that someone will perform an action, it is nothing more than a case of predictive expectation. Since it lacks any sort of moral component, we can use predictive expectation to predict the behavior of animals; someone might predict that the ducks will appear at any moment. And sometimes we can use predictive expectaion with respect to inanimate objects, as when someone forms the expectation that the fog will disappear gradually during the morning.

I will refer to these two types of expectaion as normative expectation and predictive expectation. The focus of this study will be normative expectation, and I understand this term to refer to all cases in which the expectation has a moral component. I do not say, though, that we can ignore predictive expectation for the remainder of the discussion, for sometimes we have diffilculty distinguishing the two cases.

Suppose that a child has lied when answering a question, and after a punishment is administered the child is given another opportunity to answer the same question. Someone might form the expectation that this time the child will tell the truth. The expectation might be offered as a simple prediction on the grounds that the prospect of another punishment may be repugnant to the child, but the person forming the expectation might just as easily be expressing the belief that this is what the child ought to be doing (in a sense of ought which will be discussed in Chapter Four). Thus, normative expectation and predictive expectation cannot always be neatly separated. Sometimes the boundary between them is difficult to discern.

Normative expectations are characterized by Frederick Bird and James Waters as, "Standards for behavior that are sufficiently compelling and authoritative that people feel they must either comply with them, make a show of complying with them, or offer good reasons why not (Bird and Waters, 1989, p. 74)." Although I believe that the term "must" is too strong and should be replaced with a term along the lines of "should," this definition comes reasonably close to capturing what ordinary people think of as expectations which are normative in nature. For the purposes of the ensuing discussion I will rely upon this, at least unofficially, as a definition for moral expectation. An interesting alternative account based upon the family resemblance of "expectation" is provided by Ludwig Wittgenstein (Wittgenstein, 1958, pp. 20–21).

Another category of expectations might be identified as the expectations formed about people's behavior relative to a system of rules which are non-moral in nature. A club might have a set of rules which are conditions for membership, and the rules might be framed in terms of expectations which are binding upon prospective members. For example, one rule might declare that new members are expected to attend orientation sessions. Such an expectation appears to be neither normative nor predictive in nature. The failure by a prospective member to attend orientation classes is not a moral lapse, unless perhaps the member made a promise to attend. Nothing is morally wrong as such in failing to meet a condition which the club specifies as a condition of membership. The failure will simply make the person ineligible for membership. Likewise, the expectation to attend orientation classes is not a predictive expectation. When the person in charge of the orientation sessions tells a prospective member that she is expected to attend an orientation session next Tuesday, this statement is not intended to function as a mere prediction that she will attend.

The expectations generated by rules of a non-moral nature can be described simply as rule expectations. Some normative expectations might be described as generated by the rules of morality, but the term "rules expectations" will be reserved for expectations associated with rules whose basis is non-moral. A hard and fast distinction between normative expectations and rules expectations may be difficult to establish or articulate, for deciding whether a given rule is purely a matter of convention or whether it is somehow rooted in morality is not always easy. A sign in a store might inform customers that anyone wishing to purchase alcoholic beverages is expected to produce proper identification; whether the expectation stated on the sign is moral or non-moral is possibly a matter of dispute. But I will nevertheless assume that a distinction exists, and we can recognize at least three types of expectations.

One difference between normative and rule expectations is that the language of obligation appears to be appropriate to all instances of rule expectations. Earlier I urged that some normative expectations are not obligatory in nature; we do not always have a moral obligation to do what we are morally expected to do. But when we cross from the moral to the non-moral sphere of discourse the situation appears to change. In the non-moral sphere the language of obligation can invariably be applied to the rules generating the expectations. The expectation that prospective members of a club attend orientation classes is a matter of obligation. Attending these sessions is obligatory to become members of the club. The rule demands that we attend these classes. The matter can also be stated in terms of requirements. The rules of a club or organization are requirements binding upon the members, just as moral obligations are requirements binding upon moral agents. But although some normative expectations fail to be morally required of anyone, rule expectations are invariably required of those for whom the rules apply. Nothing about such rules is optional.

That rule expectations embody requirements may help explain why people have tended to neglect the category of normative expectation. If people are accustomed to thinking about rule expectations in terms of requirements or obligations, then they may naturally think of moral expectations in terms of requirements or obligations. Thus, they might think of normative expectations in terms of moral obligations. If the expectations generated by non-moral rules function as requirements, then they might conclude that normative expectations are generated by the rules of morality and are therefore moral requirements. And, if this is true, then they may see little point in undertaking an investigation of normative expectations. If no difference between a moral obligation and a normative expectation exists, people need only understand the nature of moral obligation to understand what they need to understand about normative expectation.

People may find it natural to think that normative expectations, like rule expectations, can be described in terms of requirements. And some normative expectations can be thought of as requirements. Some normative requirements are generated by the rules of morality and are therefore moral requirements. But thinking that normative expectations in general possess this feature is mistaken. Some normative expectations are in this sense optional. The failure to carry them out constitutes a moral lapse, but it falls short of constituting a failure to do what is required of a person. Thus, some may have neglected the category of normative expectation because of an assumption about normative expectation which is mistaken.

An obvious feature about the moral life is the importance of knowing the demands of morality and living in accord with these demands. Carrying out the moral obligations which are binding upon us is of paramount importance. However, a central theme of this book is that the moral life consists of more than identifying these moral obligations and carrying them out. Beyond the scope of these moral requirements lie normative expectations which do not qualify as requirements. And while the failure to carry out or fulfil such expectations may not be as critical as the failure to carry out moral obligations, we are nevertheless advised to take them seriously. An important dimension of the moral life is to take stock of what we are morally expected to do and to carry out these moral expectations, even when they fall short of qualifying as moral obligations.

The failure to carry out what we are morally expected but not required to do is a moral failure. I will describe this type of moral failure in terms of moral blameworthiness. When a normative expectation is binding upon a moral agent, and the agent fails to carry out this expectation, the failure is deserving of moral blame. To omit carrying out what we are morally expected to do is morally blameworthy. Saying that the failure is blameworthy is not exactly the same as saying that the agent is blameworthy for this failure, for in situations where a group expectation is not fulfilled some members of the group may not personally bear moral blame for the failure. But in typical cases the agent in question is worthy of blame.

Sometimes moral expectations can apply to omissions. Just as we can be expected to perform an action, we can be expected to omit or refrain from an action. Where people who are morally expected to refrain from an action nevertheless perform the action, the performance of the action is morally blameworthy. In these cases people fail to carry out the moral expectation to refrain from action, the failure consists in the performance of an action, and the performance is rendered morally blameworthy.

The failure to carry out a normative expectation is invariably morally blameworthy, but not every failure is equally blameworthy. Blameworthiness is a concept capable of coming in degrees. The performance of some actions might be blameworthy to a very high degree, and the performance of other actions might be blameworthy to a degree close to zero. Other things being equal, the performance of an action which is morally forbidden (that is, an action which violates moral obligation) is more blameworthy than if it were not morally forbidden. But an act not morally forbidden can still be blameworthy to some degree to perform, and this is extremely important in the consideration of normative expectations. Whenever we fail to do what we are morally expected to do, the failure is morally blameworthy to at least a modest or minimal degree.

Suppose that in the opening example you decide that you are within your rights to refrain from opening the door for the woman struggling to enter. If I am correct that you are not morally obligated to open the door, your inaction does not qualify as morally forbidden and someone would be mistaken to charge that you have violated a moral obligation. Nevertheless your inaction qualifies as morally blameworthy, and for this reason your inaction is deserving of moral criticism. The degree to which your inaction is morally blameworthy is open to debate, but it is definitely blameworthy to some degree greater than zero.

One lesson to be learned from examples of this type is that the moral life asks us to do more than carry out the moral obligations binding upon us. This point has not traditionally received a great deal of emphasis in the moral literature. Traditionally moral obligation together with the closely related notion of moral responsibility (and the precise relation between these two notions need not be pursued here) have figured most prominently in discussions of morality. Discussions of rights have also tended to fit into this picture, for rights are frequently cashed out in terms of obligations and responsibilities. Moral agents are frequently considered to be within their rights to do something if no moral obligations or responsibilities to the contrary exist.

To focus, as so many people do, upon what we are within our rights to do or refrain from doing, is to lead us to an impoverished view of morality. A person pursuing this narrow focus will presumably be diligent about not violating obligations and responsibilities but will remain ignorant about satisfying moral expectations which go beyond these. If everything we consider important is a matter of doing what we are within our rights to do, we will not be likely to assist others and we may not be concerned for the welfare or needs of others. But precisely here normative expectation becomes relevant. Many of our normative expectations are directed to assisting others, and the failure to do so is a moral failure.

A key emphasis of moral education is that we take account of the interests and needs of other people. Children are routinely taught that, in addition to pursuing their own self interests, assisting others in the pursuit of their interests is good. Frequently we are in a position to assist others in ways that they cannot easily or conveniently assist themselves, and assisting them is a good thing independently of the good effects it may have for ourselves. But when ethical theory is fixated upon obligations, responsibilities, and rights it does not provide a congenial setting for this type of emphasis. For while we occasionally have obligations and responsibilities to assist others (and lack the corresponding right to refrain from doing so), many other occasions present themselves when we should act for the sake of others even though morality does not demand that we do so. I believe that an emphasis upon normative expectation helps to fill this gap. It helps to show us that ignoring the needs of others can be morally wrong in ways that cannot be explained by appealing just to obligations, responsibilities, and rights.

In addition, and perhaps more importantly, it provides a reason or motivation for altruistic action that goes beyond the reasons provided by some of the traditional approaches to ethics. Why should a person go out of his or her way to assist someone else, possibly a total stranger? The approach of a Kantian might be to appeal to some type of moral duty, the approach of an act utilitarian might be to appeal to consequences which we have an obligation to realize or bring about, the approach of a divine command theorist might be to appeal to the commands of a deity which we are obligated to honor, and so forth. But a different kind of reason motivates someone who takes seriously the expectations of morality: We are simply expected to do so, independently of any talk of duties and obligations. We are expected to see ways in which we can be of assistance to those around us and to act accordingly. This is a simple idea, one which may hark back to our moral instruction as children, but it is an idea which tends to be somewhat foreign to traditional approaches to ethical theory.

In recent years a revival of interest in virtue ethics has drawn some attention away from the central emphasis upon notions such as obligations, responsibilities, and rights. And the work produced by those articulating the place of virtue and vice in morality has greatly enriched people's awareness of what is involved in living the moral life. Virtue ethics arguably helps to fill some of the gaps in the moral life which are left unfilled by traditional approaches, and the dimension of the moral life addressed by virtue ethics is indispensable. That a complete moral theory contains attention both to the deontic and the aretaic dimensions of morality is becoming a commonly accepted idea among moral theorists. Neither can be entirely sacrificed for the sake of the other.

But we would be mistaken to conclude from this observation that virtue ethics fills in these gaps in a manner which makes attention to moral expectations unnecessary. Moral expectation is primarily a deontic, not an aretaic notion. It is a notion concerned with the rightness and wrongness of particular actions. It is not first and foremost concerned with the development of dispositions or character traits. An awareness of and response to moral expectations should take place alongside a development of virtue, but neither is a substitute for the other. Moral expectation addresses aspects of morality also addressed by traditional deontic notions in ways that enlarge the scope of these notions, while virtue ethics addresses aspects of morality which go beyond what the deontic notions are designed to capture.

Saying that moral expectation is primarily a deontic notion leaves open the possibility that in some circumstances moral expectations fall within the realm of virtue ethics. We can form an expectation that someone develop a particular virtue or have a particular virtue, and we can form an expectation that someone resist developing or having a particular vice. If a person can be expected to develop a particular virtue such as courage or to resist developing a particular vice such as greed, the expectation in question is not deontic in form. It is not aimed directly at the performance or omission of various actions. Instead, it is an expectation which is aimed at the development of dispositions or traits which embody the virtue of courage or resistance to greed. If such moral expectations are possible, and I believe they are, then the scope of moral expectation is not entirely separate from the scope of virtue ethics.

Moral expectation occupies an important middle ground between what is morally required of us and what is morally neutral (an act is morally neutral if and only if it is neither morally obligatory, forbidden, praiseworthy, nor blameworthy). Because traditional moral theory has focused upon the requirements of morality, this middle ground has not always received the attention it deserves. People have a tendency to think that once they have discharged their moral obligations and responsibilities, everything else is optional and they are entitled to indulge themselves in a state of moral relaxation. The tendency is to think that beyond this point they need not engage in behavior having a positive moral status.

By now we should see that this way of thinking is mistaken. A recognition that some acts can rightly be expected though not required of us can be important for ordinary people in thinking about how to live a moral life. People need to understand that they are open to moral blame when they fail to carry out their moral expectations. The moral ground between what is required of them and what is morally neutral includes many of the areas of life in which we carry out our deliberations and decisions. As already observed, many decisions concerning the needs and interests of others find their place in this area of the moral terrain. The decision to be of assistance to another may not be morally required of us, and yet the decision is not necessarily a morally neutral decision. Some type of negative moral status can attach to a person who refrains from assisting another, and this is a fact about the moral life which is important for people to realize. In one way or another this is a theme which resonates throughout the subsequent chapters of this book. Following are brief synopses of these chapters.

In the next chapter I argue that people sometimes form false moral expectations about themselves or others, and sometimes a person is morally expected to perform an act even though no one has an expectation that the person perform the act. Thus, it is neither a necessary nor sufficient condition of a person's being expected to perform an act that someone have an expectation that the person perform the act. Nevertheless, these facts should in no way cause us to take a dismissive attitude toward either the advice received from others or towards expectations which no one has articulated.

Chapter Three surveys what philosophers have said about moral expectation. Although none of these philosophers has produced any type of sustained examination of the topic, some have made reference to it in ways that are important and insightful. The survey in this chapter is divided into three areas. First, many speak about expectation in terms of reasonable expectation and have commented on what moral agents can be reasonably expected to do. Second, some writers have spoken about the sociological factors by which moral expectations are frequently shaped. Third, several writers have commented upon the negative moral status which attaches to the failure to carry out moral expectations.

The topic of Chapter Four is the relationship between what people ought to do and what they are morally expected to do. In recent years several writers have distinguished between the ought of moral duty and a weaker type of moral ought. Although the scope of non-obligatory moral expectation does not exactly coincide with the scope of the weak ought, examining this class of actions is beneficial. One benefit lies in distinguishing between strong and weak versions of the ought implies can principle and formulating a parallel type of principle which governs moral expectation.

In Chapter Five moral expectation is analyzed in the context of agreements made by two or more people. Whenever people enter into agreements expectations are created, and whenever people dissolve agreements expectations are terminated or otherwise altered. Often these expectations are moral in nature. In this chapter the role of moral expectation is explored in the following five types of situations: The proposal to enter into an agreement, the proposal to dissolve an agreement, the refusal to enter into an agreement, the refusal to dissolve an agreement, and the opposition to the formation or termination of an agreement by a third party.

Frequently people attempt to avoid moral expectation. In Chapter Six two ways of avoiding moral expectation are distinguished. When we escape from a moral expectation we manage to alter the expectation so that it no longer attaches to us, at least not in its present form. We can also eliminate an expectation entirely or eliminate the possibility of an expectation before it comes into existence. The partial avoidance of a moral expectation consists in avoiding some but not all of what is necessary to bring it about. In this context a distinction is introduced between the bare fulfillment of an expectation and a more robust fulfillment in which someone goes beyond the call of expectation.

In Chapter Seven I argue that groups of two or more agents can be morally expected to bring about or refrain from bringing about a state of affairs. Sometimes the fulfillment of the expectation requires that all members of the group perform actions, but this is not always the case. This chapter explores a variety of possibilities for satisfying these expectations. When a group expectation is not fulfilled, the members of the group sometimes bear equal blame for the failure. But some factors are analyzed which can cause some members to bear more blame for the failure than others.

The symbolic dimension of moral expectation is the topic of Chapter Eight. The first part of this chapter introduces and explains the notion of the symbolic value of an act, developed by Robert Nozick. The second part explores the notion as it bears upon acts which embody or manifest moral expectation. Fulfilling a moral expectation, verbalizing a moral expectation, refusing to carry out a moral expectation, promising to fulfil a moral expectation, and carrying the wrong moral expectation are all acts which can take on symbolic value.

Chapter Nine explores the relation between moral expectation and acts which are morally blameworthy but not obligatory. These include what Roderick Chisholm and Ernest Sosa refer to as acts of offence, what Julia Driver calls suberogatory acts, and acts grounded in what Michael J. Zimmerman calls accuses. All such acts are clearly related to the failure of non-obligatory moral expectation. Accordingly, the work of these philosophers makes possible a deepened appreciation of the consequences involved in failing to take our moral expectations seriously.

The expectations of God are discussed in Chapter Ten. If human beings are capable of forming non-obligatory moral expectations, we can plausibly judge that God possesses this capability. Thus, God can discourage human behavior (namely, the failure to carry out such expectations) he does not explicitly forbid. Such a claim does not appear to square with the views of the Protestant Reformers. This chapter also examines the views of some contemporary theists such as Alan Donagan and Eleonore Stump whose views do not appear to accommodate the idea that God discourages behavior he does not forbid.

The concluding chapter attempts to provide some insight into how moral expectation operates in the context of people's professional lives. The first part examines some moral expectations which attach to members of organizations in their role as employees. The second part describes three important lessons which can be learned when they make an effort to take these expectations seriously. The final part consists of practical advice regarding the manner in which people should approach their moral expectations in the workplace.

Two

FAULTY AND UNFORMED EXPECTATIONS

From the earliest of ages we learn that certain behavior is morally expected of us. We learn of certain things we are expected to do and certain things we are expected to refrain from doing. In early childhood these expectations are conveyed primarily by our parents or caretakers, but when we are children we may learn about what we are expected to do from a variety of other people. These others might include grandparents, siblings, and friends. Once we begin to attend school, our teachers are significant conveyors of information regarding what is expected of us.

As we grow older the necessity of learning from others what we are expected to do or refrain from doing diminishes. We are less dependent upon others for coming to know which expectations attach to our behavior. Part of the explanation for this phenomenon is that we acquire the ability to have or entertain expectations regarding our own behavior. Thus, not only do other people have expectations about our behavior; we come to have expectations about our own future behavior (Miller, 2001, p. 132).

The expectations we have about our own behavior are frequently shaped by the expectations others have about us. Suppose the parents of a young child have regularly conveyed the expectation that the child keep his bedroom neat. When the child becomes older he may have the expectation about himself that he keep his bedroom neat. Of course, this is probably not an example of a moral expectation. But the same applies to moral expectations. We come to have expectations regarding our own moral conduct, and these expectations are often shaped or influenced by the expectations others have expressed about our behavior in the past.

Frequently we learn what we are expected to do when others articulate these expectations in a manner which makes explicit mention of an expectation. For example, when a family acquires a new pet, a child in the family might be told, "You are expected to treat this animal with respect." However, we learn what is expected of us in a variety of other ways. The statements, "You better treat this animal with respect" or "You know you should treat this animal with respect" will likely convey the same message to a child as the original statement.

Unspoken gestures even seem to have the capability of conveying expectations to us. Suppose a child comes to admire a neighbor's brand new sports car, and the child climbs into the driver's seat, pretending to drive the car. The neighbor walks over to the car and, without saying a word, gestures with a brisk movement of his outstretched thumb to signify that the child is expected to leave the car. Through observing this gesture the child may learn that leaving the car is what is expected of him. In other types of situations people operate with unspoken "background expectations" about the behavior of themselves or others (Cullity, 1997, p. 117).

Sometimes we find out what is expected of us by others at times when we are not in contact with others. A message left on voice mail can inform someone that he or she is expected to attend a particular meeting. During a severe drought an announcement on the radio might inform someone that the residents of the local community are expected to use water as sparingly as possible. Someone else might acquire this bit of information by reading the newspaper. And clearly we can imagine many other examples in which expectations are communicated in the absence of personal contact.

The previous chapter made clear that moral obligation composes a sub-category of moral expectation. We are morally expected to do everything we are morally obligated to do, but the reverse is not the case. What has been said here about learning what is expected of us applies then to moral obligation and to other types of expectations. Some of what others claim to be morally expected of us is obligatory, and on occasion we learn about behavior that is required of us. We learn that morality has its demands and that some of these demands are binding upon us as individuals. Some things are required of us to do, and other things are required of us to refrain from doing. For example, we learn that we are morally required to refrain from taking the life of another human being, because taking the life of another is morally forbidden.

Generally speaking, we learn that honoring our moral obligations is a serious matter. Nothing is optional about carrying out our moral obligations. If anything about morality needs to be taken seriously, it is doing what we are morally required to do. To do otherwise is forbidden.

Among many people is a general sense that not everything which is morally expected of us takes the form of an iron-clad requirement. Not everything which is morally expected of us is an outright moral demand whose failure to carry out is morally forbidden. The expectation to assist another person to whom we have no strong attachments will not strike most people as something morality demands of us. It is something others can rightly expect us to do, but most people would not see it as something we are required to do (although someone might hold the view that we are required to assist other people at some time or other). We might lack the ability to draw a clear distinction between the expectations which qualify as requirements and those that do not, but the general sense that such a distinction exists is probably widespread.

Although we frequently learn about our moral expectations from other people, we also discover that the expectations others have about us are sometimes mistaken. People sometimes form a moral expectation that we perform an action which we cannot rightly be expected to perform. In other words, people can form mistaken moral expectations about moral agents. From the fact that

someone has a moral expectation that a person perform a given act, the proposition that the person can rightly be expected to perform it does not follow.
People can form faulty moral expectations. (To say that someone "forms" a
moral expectation should not be taken to imply that the person is creating a
moral expectation; if such an expectation exists, it should be taken to imply that
the person consciously recognizes or affirms its existence.)

Sometimes faulty moral expectations are the result of faulty information
possessed by the person forming the expectation. A man on the beach might be
mistaken by others to be the lifeguard, and they might form a moral expectation
that he perform a dangerous rescue. But this does not entail that he can rightly
be expected to perform the rescue. Their expectation concerning him is based
upon misinformation. Sometimes faulty information about the action to be performed can lead to faulty expectations. Someone might form the expectation
that the lifeguard perform a dangerous rescue. But the rescue in question might
be so dangerous that it is beyond the capability of a trained lifeguard, and in this
case the lifeguard cannot rightly be expected to perform the rescue. If the person forming the expectation is unaware that the rescue is this dangerous, then
the faulty expectation is based upon mistaken information about the action to
be performed.

In other cases faulty expectations can be the result of factors concerning
the relationship between the person forming the expectations and the person
about whom the expectations are made. Suppose that two people come to have
different perceptions about the nature of their romantic involvement. One person might regard a second person as a casual friend, while the latter regards the
former as a serious romantic interest. On this basis, the second person might
form the expectation that the other not have any other romantic interests. But to
say that the first person can rightly be expected to refrain from romantic relationships with others is not plausible.

Faulty expectations can also arise when one person forms expectations
concerning another which he or she simply has no right to form. An employer,
for example, is not entitled to expect that her employees will paint her house or
run personal errands for her. In addition, Annette Baier argues that a person
who employs threats or force to sustain a trusting relationship has no right to
expect trustworthiness on the part of those who are threatened or forced (Baier,
1986, p. 255). So if persons employing threats nevertheless form such expectations, they might well be mistaken.

The picture which emerges from these considerations can be described as
follows. Upon learning that others form moral expectations concerning our behavior, we frequently regard this behavior as something that can be morally
expected of us. Moreover, we regard the fact that it can be morally expected of
us as a reason for undertaking the behavior. But we know that the moral expectations others express concerning our behavior are not always rightly expected
of us. While their expressions of expectations are important guides to the dis-

covery of what is morally expected of us, we are mindful that they are not infallible guides. Thus, while hearing others express moral expectations concerning our behavior is important, we also need to ascertain that which can rightly be morally expected of us.

Forming faulty moral expectations about our own behavior is even possible. People who form expectations about themselves based upon lofty ideals or the emulation of the lives of saints may simply be unable to live up to these lofty expectations. These expectations will then turn out to be mistaken expectations, because we cannot rightly be expected to do that which is not within our powers to do (more on this point in Chapter Four). Often we lack knowledge about our future ability to carry out the expectations we have about ourselves. In many ways we may find that expectations we formed about ourselves at various times in the past are expectations which cannot possibly be true. We are no less fallible in forming expectations regarding ourselves than in forming expectations regarding other people.

To summarize, we come to know what is morally expected of us by hearing others express moral expectations about us. Some of these expectations are moral in nature, and some of these moral expectations take the form of moral obligations. We are required to carry out our moral obligations, but we are not required to carry out other types of moral expectations. Sometimes we form moral expectations about our own future behavior, and these are frequently modeled after the expectations others form about us. Finally, the moral expectations people form about others or themselves are not always true. We can form faulty expectations about others or about ourselves.

On the basis of what has so far been shown, we can conclude that the formation of moral expectations about us by others or by ourselves is not a sufficient condition of our having these moral expectations. Since the formation of a moral expectation that a person perform a particular action can be false, it does not suffice to establish the fact that the person can rightly be expected to perform the action.

In what follows I will argue that the formation of moral expectations about us is also not a necessary condition of our having these moral expectations. It is not a necessary condition of our being morally expected to perform an act that someone actually forms a moral expectation that we perform the act. In other words, a person can be expected to perform an action even though no one has ever formed an expectation, either explicitly or implicitly, that the person perform the action. We would be mistaken to insist that a moral agent is morally expected to do only that which people expect him or her to do (and here the discussion is limited to human beings and is not intended to hold true with respect to divine beings).

The first argument to show that the existence of moral expectations is not dependent upon the existence of an expectation formed by someone appeals to the fact that some moral expectations are expectations to omit or refrain from acting. Just as we can be expected to perform actions, we can be expected to omit or refrain from various actions. A moment's reflection will show that we can be morally expected to refrain from performing vast numbers of actions. As many evil actions are possible to perform, we are morally expected to refrain from them. Consider a moral agent named Sam. For every living human being, Sam is morally expected to refrain from murdering this human being. But surely no one has taken the trouble of recognizing such a vast number of expectations about Sam. There are myriad ways that Sam can go about performing evil actions, and to think that someone, including Sam, could form moral expectations about every one of these evil actions would be ludicrous.

A second argument concerns cases in which something debilitating happens to the only person who has formed a moral expectation about another. Suppose Sam's employer has formed an expectation about Sam's behaving ethically in the workplace and that no one else, including Sam, has this expectation. One day Sam's employer dies, and now no one expects this behavior of Sam. The new employer is not concerned about the moral climate of the workplace. Would it make sense for Sam to feel a sense of relief that he is no longer expected to behave ethically in the workplace? He may feel a sense of relief that no longer is someone present in the workplace to monitor his behavior, but for him to believe that the expectation itself has vanished would be unreasonable.

We would be mistaken to believe that expectations attaching to our behavior vanish when the people who have formed them perish (or become comatose, victims of dementia, or whatever). Surely expectations do not perish with the people who have formed them. And the same would hold true if Sam were able to persuade his old employer to give up this expectation. If Sam could rightly be expected to demonstrate ethical behavior in the workplace, the persuasion of his employer to give up the expectation would certainly not be enough to put an end to the expectation. Moral expectations are not so fragile that they cannot exist apart from the persons who have formed them.

A third argument in support of this conclusion concerns the relationship between moral expectation and moral obligation. Earlier I argued that every moral obligation is a moral expectation, a point which has also been noted in the literature (Williams, 1985, p. 187). And if this is true, then what is not a necessary condition of moral obligation cannot qualify as a necessary condition of moral expectation. Is a necessary condition of moral obligation that a person form a moral expectation that the moral agent in question carry out the obligation? Is Sam's moral obligation to perform a particular action dependent upon a person forming the expectation that Sam perform this action?

These questions are to be answered in the negative. The view that moral obligation cannot exist apart from a (human) person forming moral expectations of the requisite sort is not plausible. Controversy abounds regarding the nature of moral obligations and their place in morality, but this view is completely at odds with common sense. And if the existence of a person forming moral expectations is not a necessary condition of moral obligation, then it cannot be a necessary condition of moral expectation. For if moral obligations can exist apart from a person forming moral expectations, then the same holds true of moral expectation.

On the basis of these arguments I conclude that the existence of persons forming moral expectations is neither a necessary nor sufficient condition of the existence of moral expectations. Just as we find ourselves with moral obligations, the same is true of moral expectation in general. We simply find that we can rightly be expected to engage in certain types of behavior, regardless of the expectations formed by ourselves or others. Sometimes what people expect us to do is simply mistaken, and sometimes no one expects us to do what we are in fact rightly expected to do.

Having put forth these arguments, I hasten to reaffirm the importance of hearing people express moral expectations regarding our behavior. Essential to the process of moral education is taking note of what they say, taking what they say to heart, and developing the capacity to form moral expectations regarding our own behavior. As in all avenues of life, we find that people make mistaken judgments. But this is scarcely a suitable reason to develop a dismissive attitude toward what others say, and in no way have the arguments put forth here been intended to encourage such an attitude. Naturally, some people will strike us as more credible than others as bearers of judgments regarding what is expected of us, and we react accordingly. But a basic spirit of credulity regarding what others say in this regard should not be discouraged.

In addition, we should take our moral expectations seriously, whether or not anyone has taken the trouble to form them. Developing a dismissive attitude toward moral expectations that no one happens to have formed regarding what we should or should not do would be wrong. We may be tempted to dismiss these expectations because they are burdensome and interfere with our freedom to live as we see fit. We might reason that being constrained by the moral expectations others have formed is bad enough and that adding to the burden by acknowledging additional moral expectations would be unbearable.

Clearly such reasoning is faulty. Whether or not we acknowledge a moral expectation does not determine whether the moral expectation is real. We simply have moral expectations, regardless of what others (or ourselves) have thought or said, and we can know what they are apart from being told by others or having formed them ourselves. Perhaps our moral expectations are burdensome, and they undeniably feel burdensome on occasion, but to pretend they do not exist is nothing other than being morally irresponsible.

Some might have trouble with the notion that moral expectation exists apart from what people have thought or believed or communicated. Perhaps the idea that acts can be expected of someone in the absence of anyone who has formed expectations of him or her may seem odd. Here it is helpful to note that parallel situations are common in moral discourse. A praiseworthy act need not actually be recognized by someone as worthy of praise. To say that an act is praiseworthy is to say that it achieves a standard of conduct which makes it worthy of praise.

In like manner, to say that an act can be morally expected of a person is to say that it achieves a standard of conduct which makes it worthy of someone's forming an expectation that the person perform the act. When I form an expectation that my children treat their teachers with respect, the expectation I form is attaching itself to a standard of conduct which does not depend upon the formation of my expectation for being the standard that it is. The standard of conduct is what it is regardless of what I or anyone else thinks or says. Moral expectation is not logically bound to there being actual instances of people forming moral expectations. Actual instances are neither necessary nor sufficient for there being moral expectations with regard to a particular person and a particular course of action.

The parallel between praiseworthy acts and morally expected acts may not satisfy everyone. Some may find room for raising additional doubts of a skeptical nature as to whether moral expectations are real independently of actual human persons. Just as some moral skeptics ask whether moral obligation is real, some may wonder the same about moral expectation. A skeptic can challenge the idea that actions can be morally expected of a person, over and above the moral expectations that various people form of that person.

I know of no perfect way of responding to this skeptical challenge. The best that can be done is to point out that people, upon hearing others give expression to moral expectations concerning them, sometimes regard them as being right and sometimes regard them as being mistaken in expecting the behavior. Thus, people widely acknowledge a truth to the matter as to whether we can be expected to behave as morally expected, just as they acknowledge a truth to the matter as to whether we have a moral obligation to behave in some particular manner.

A moral skeptic will not be persuaded by such reasoning, but we should recognize that the concept of moral expectation functions in the common reasoning of people as something more than just a matter of opinion or speculation. As such it provides a significant reason for acting. That certain actions can be morally expected of us appears to be commonly taken for granted, just as moral agents take for granted that certain actions are morally required of them.

A milder version of skepticism concerning moral expectation takes the following form. A skeptic might grant that our moral expectations are real in the sense that we can rightly be expected to perform or refrain from performing some acts. Thus, a skeptic might acknowledge a truth to the matter as to whether a person can be morally expected to behave in a particular manner. Nevertheless, he or she might go on to deny that we have any reliable or dependable access to such truth and consequently see little point paying attention to our moral expectations. If two people disagree about the moral expectations which apply to one of them and if neither has any reliable way to access the truth of the matter, pursuing the matter may seem pointless.

This brand of moral skepticism is epistemological in nature. It challenges our ability to know what we are morally expected to do. If we cannot access the truth about moral expectations with any reliability, then the ability to have knowledge regarding them is dubious. For knowledge about something presupposes the ability to have adequate warrant or justification about our beliefs concerning it. If we cannot access the truth about moral expectations with reliability, then we cannot apparently progress beyond mere beliefs or opinions regarding them.

As with the skeptic who challenges the idea that moral expectations can exist apart from the persons forming them, we have no perfect response to the challenge of the more moderate skeptic. Establishing a convincing argument that human beings have the ability to apprehend or intuit the truths of morality, let alone providing an account of how this apprehension works, is notoriously difficult. And those who are predisposed to be skeptical of such an ability will be particularly difficult to convince.

Nevertheless, in the absence of a knock-down argument to refute the skeptic, we can draw a distinction between the claim that we have no reliable access to truths about moral expectations and the claim that we have no perfectly reliable access to truths about moral expectations. The latter claim is surely true, as evidenced by the fact that people are sometimes mistaken in the judgments they make about moral expectations. Our access to these truths is anything but perfectly reliable. But the claim that we have no reliable access to these truths is a far more radical claim, and surely we can challenge the skeptic regarding this claim.

If the skeptic is correct that we have no reliable access to truths about moral expectations, then we have no knowledge regarding these expectations and we must rely upon beliefs and opinions to ascertain how we are expected to conduct ourselves. But surely this view is open to challenge. When a child is told by a parent what he or she is expected to do, we can most certainly presume that the parent knows what the child is expected to do and that by communicating this expectation, the child is now in a position to know as well. Moral education rests upon the presumption that what is being communicated to children is knowledge. The whole idea that a child learns what is expected of him or her does not make sense if we cannot go beyond having mere beliefs or opinions about the subject.

Suppose that as a child Sam is told by his parents that he is expected to treat other people with respect, and Sam acquires the belief that this expectation applies to his behavior. Is Sam now in a position to know that he is expected to treat other people with respect? I believe that few would answer this question in the negative. For few would question that Sam has learned from his parents that he is expected to treat other people with respect. And if Sam learns this from his parents, then the idea that no one possesses reliable access to the truth about moral expectations is false.

The process may be different for younger children. As a young child Sam may have thought of expectations as relative to the persons expressing them. He may have been aware that his mother expected one thing, his father another thing, and so on. Then at a certain age Sam may have achieved the ability to recognize a truth to the matter about what he is expected to do.

The skeptic, naturally, is happy to deny that people have the ability to learn about their moral expectations and that moral education is even possible. And this position might have an initial plausibility. But we need to remember that moral obligation is a species of moral expectation, and this realization may remove some of the initial plausibility of the skeptical view. To deny that people have the capability of teaching others what their moral obligations are is difficult, and to deny that people have the capability of learning what moral duties or obligations are binding upon them is likewise difficult. And if moral education regarding our moral duties or obligations does not exist, what is left to constitute the content of moral education?

A person who doubts the possibility of knowledge concerning moral expectations is committed to doubting the possibility of having knowledge regarding our moral duties and obligations. Moreover, someone who questions the possibility of moral education regarding our moral expectations is committed to doubting the possibility of moral education regarding our moral duties and obligations. But to entertain such doubts about our duties or obligations is implausible. To deny that we can know what we are morally obligated to do or to deny that others can teach us what we are morally obligated to do flies in the face of common sense. By the same token, to deny that we can know what we are morally expected to do or to deny that others can teach us what we are morally expected to do is implausible.

To summarize, two ways of expressing skepticism regarding moral expectations are to challenge the idea that they are real (in the sense that statements about people having them can be true) and to challenge the idea that we have any reliable access to truths about moral expectations. While we have no perfect way of responding to either skeptical position, we can challenge these positions. The first can be called into question by observing that it is totally at odds with the way people think and talk about moral expectations. In common discourse people almost invariably assume that when others express moral expectations about their behavior what these others say is either right or wrong. People take for granted that a truth to the matter exists about whether we can be expected to behave as others expect us to behave.

The second skeptical position, that truths about moral expectations exist but we have no reliable access to them, is also a position which eludes a knockdown refutation. However, its implausibility begins to become apparent when we see that this position precludes having knowledge about moral expectations or being able to teach others about their moral expectations. And its implausibility becomes even more apparent upon seeing that it precludes having knowledge of our moral obligations or the possibility of moral education about moral obligation.

In conclusion, we can reasonably suppose that the manner in which moral expectation is spoken of in common discourse is not grossly mistaken. People routinely assume that judgments about moral expectations have a truth value, people routinely assume that they can know these judgments when true, and people routinely assume that they can teach these truths to others. I believe that people are warranted in making these routine assumptions. The account of moral expectation I develop in this book affirms that people's ordinary intuitions about their moral expectations and about moral expectation in general, while not infallible, are reliable enough to use as guides to living. Others may sometimes be mistaken when they form expectations about our behavior, but we would be foolish to think that no value can be found in listening to what they say and attempting to apply what they say to our lives.

Three

REASONABLE, SOCIAL, AND FAILED EXPECTATIONS

This chapter surveys some of what has been said about moral expectation by philosophers. Although none of these individuals has focussed specifically upon moral expectation or produced any type of sustained survey or examination of the topic, many philosophers have made reference to it. Just as people refer to moral expectation in ordinary conversation, it is frequently mentioned in the philosophical literature.

My aim is not to produce an exhaustive list of what philosophers have said about moral expectation, for much of what philosophers have said is no more illuminating or insightful than what is said in ordinary conversation. Instead, my aim is to conduct a survey which will help shed genuine light upon the topic and upon the ensuing discussion in this book. Further, my aim is to do more than produce a tedious listing of references or quotations; I will attempt to discover and highlight common themes in what various philosophers have said and, where appropriate, to offer commentary on what they say.

Three common themes from the literature which can profitably be explored are reasonable expectation, social expectation, and the failure of expectation. Several writers have commented on what we can reasonably be expected to do. Although what we can reasonably be expected to do is not exactly the same as what we can rightly be expected to do, their insights will prove instructive. The discussion also includes several other philosophers who have characterized expectation in ways closely related to reasonable expectation.

Second, some writers have noted that our moral expectations are frequently shaped by sociological factors. Roughly speaking, we are more likely to be expected to benefit others to whom we have close ties than those to whom we do not. Some develop this idea by appealing to the concept of partiality. Others who have commented on social expectations focus upon notions such as community or the effectiveness of solving social problems, and some approach expectation as relative to social systems or our roles in society.

Third, several writers have emphasized that a negative moral status attaches to the failure to carry out what can rightly be expected of us. Earlier I characterized this failure in terms of moral blame; this failure is always morally blameworthy to at least a small degree. Other writers describe it as a moral defect, something for which someone is culpable, or as a type of evil. But the basic idea is the same: a negative moral status inevitably attaches to the failure to do what we can rightly be expected to do.

I begin this survey, then, by directing attention to several philosophers who approach the subject by making reference to what people can be "reasonably expected" to do. These philosophers draw their inspiration from historical figures as far back as antiquity. Aristotle, for example, declares in the *Nicomachean Ethics* (1135b 17–18) that when an injury takes place contrary to reasonable expectation, it is a "misadventure" (and when it does not and also does not involve vice it is a "mistake"). Thus, a person who could not reasonably be expected to know that his or her actions will bring about injury can be said to be the cause of a misadventure.

Suppose that a man dressed in the costume of a soldier from the Civil War is walking down the street and causes a staring cyclist to ride into a parked automobile. No one could reasonably expect the man who is walking to have foreseen the possibility of this state of affairs, and hence the outcome is a misadventure for which he presumably bears no blame. Aristotle's point appears plausible. When a person cannot reasonably foresee that his or her actions will cause an injury, the outcome is nothing more than a misadventure.

Among twentieth-century philosophers the concept of reasonable expectation finds expression in the writings of David Lyons, Claudia Card, and Bernard Williams. In speaking about the benefits we derive from the restraints imposed by law and the dependency of the system on the obedience and cooperation of one another, Lyons remarks that those who obey and respect the law form the reasonable expectation that we will reciprocate in kind (Lyons, 1984, p. 212). Since others demonstrate respect for the law, we can be reasonably expected to do the same. And he adds that we will be regarded by others as freeloaders if we fail to do so.

Card, in a discussion of whether one ever deserves to suffer on the basis of one's character, arrives at the following criterion. "A person deserves to suffer, on the whole, no more than one could reasonably be expected to suffer from another or others were he to live in a community in which everyone else had the same. . .sort of over-all character (Card, 1972, p. 185)." Thus, if authorities are considering the imposition of penalties upon someone because of a character defect, they should consider whether the penalties would be appropriate in a society where everyone had the same character defect. For example, to expect that someone be put into prison just because he is a pathological liar would be unreasonable, since to do so in a society where everyone is a pathological liar would be unreasonable. Like Lyons, Card looks to the inter-personal dynamics within society as the arena in which reasonable expectation finds its natural place.

Williams speaks about reasonable expectation in his well-known essay, "Morality, the Peculiar Institution." In a discussion of moral obligation he declares that obligation works to secure reliability, and he characterizes reliability as, "a state of affairs in which people can reasonably expect others to behave in some ways and not in others (Williams, 1985, p. 187)." The presence of moral obligation creates a stable environment in which people can reasonably expect others to act in certain ways. We can always be morally expected to carry out our moral obligations, but I believe Williams is saying more than this. Just as Lyons sees the presence of law as creating an environment in which people form reasonable expectations about one another, Williams believes moral obligation is capable of playing a similar role. It works to secure a system characterized by the kind of reliability which makes the formation of reasonable expectations possible.

Sometimes philosophers speak in terms of what can be reasonably expected of a virtuous person (Irwin, 1997, p. 210). When the scope of discourse is narrowed to those who are virtuous the reliability discussed by Williams can presumably be achieved with minimal difficulty, for a community of virtuous moral agents will be more likely to create a stable environment in which people can reasonably expect others to act in certain ways.

Although paradigm instances of reasonable expectation may arise in societal or large group settings, some cases of reasonable expectation occur in situations involving as few as two persons. Samuel C. Rickless describes an example in which a person starts up his neighbor's furnace. He believes that if the person starts up the neighbor's furnace on a regular basis, then the neighbor can reasonably expect him to do so in the future (Rickless, 1997, p. 559). The regularity of his starting up the furnace in the past can give rise to a reasonable expectation that he will do the same in the future.

What we can reasonably be expected to do is not precisely the same as what we can rightly be expected to do. Suppose that a man is sitting at a desk with a telephone in a public place when a crime is suddenly committed. Another man standing near the desk could reasonably expect the man at the desk to pick up the telephone and inform law enforcement authorities of the crime. But if the telephone were not in working order and if no other telephone were available, then he could not rightly be expected to notify the authorities by telephone. Not everything that can be reasonably expected of a person can be rightly expected of the person.

In contrary fashion, not everything that can rightly be expected of a person by an observer can be reasonably expected of the person by the observer. Suppose, as before, that a man is sitting at a desk in a public place when a crime is suddenly committed. In this scenario no telephone is on the desk, and hence the man standing near the desk cannot reasonably expect the man at the desk to find a telephone to notify the authorities. Nevertheless, the man at the desk happens to have a cell phone in his pocket, and this clearly alters the situation. In this scenario the man at the desk can rightly be expected to notify the authorities of the crime. Moreover, someone who knew about his cell phone could reasonably expect him to place a call. But the man standing near the desk can rightly expect him to place a call, even though he cannot reasonably expect him to place a call.

James Fishkin raises a point about moral expectation directly related to these issues. Recall the case in which Kitty Genovese is brutally assaulted in front of the Kew Gardens housing complex. Many of the residents hear her crying out, and at least thirty eight people look out their windows. But not a single one notifies the police in the half hour it takes for Kitty Genovese to die. Regarding this case Fishkin remarks that although a deaf-mute could not be expected to notify the police, we would expect any "ordinary" member of this group to do so (Fishkin, 1982, p. 31). Thus, he believes, talking about what can "ordinarily" be expected of people makes sense. People witnessing a crime could ordinarily be expected to notify the police, but exceptions would be made for those who are deaf-mutes. And presumably the same would hold true for those without telephones in working order. Thus, Fishkin's use of the term "ordinarily expected" appears to imply reasonable expectation. If a person can in Fishkin's sense be ordinarily expected to perform an action, then perhaps the person can reasonably be expected to perform it.

Fishkin contrasts ordinary expectation with obligation (*Ibid.*). The principles which govern general obligation, he believes, govern what can be demanded of anyone by anyone. If we are under a general obligation to refrain from murder, then it can be demanded of any of us that we refrain from murder. But ordinary expectation admits of exceptions, as we have seen, and so Fishkin appears to be in agreement with the thesis stated in Chapter One that some moral expectations fall outside the boundaries of moral obligation. For him the key factor distinguishing ordinary expectations from general obligation (in addition to the fact that obligations are demands) is the possibility that certain people are exempt from them. He does, nevertheless, leave open the possibility that some moral obligations other than general obligations do not apply to all persons.

Henry Sidgwick in *The Methods of Ethics* speaks of "normal expectations" which people form about the behavior of others. Like the ordinary expectations of Fishkin, they too admit of exceptions. Sidgwick mentions three ways in which normal expectations arise. They are based upon "definite engagements" (by which he appears to mean definite arrangements), some "vague mutual understanding," or "are merely such as an average man would form from past experience of the conduct of other men (Sidgwick, 1981, p. 442)." An example of the first would be a promise I am expected to keep. In this regard J. L. Mackie states that the institution of promising is embedded in and reinforced by "general social expectations" (Mackie, 1977, p. 81). An example of the second may be the expectation that I assist my co-worker when he begins to encounter difficulty lifting a heavy object by himself. Even though he does not request my help, we are aware of a vague mutual understanding that people should come to the aid of a co-worker who begins to encounter difficulty. An example of the third might be the expectation that I keep the lawn mowed of the house which I have just purchased, because I have observed from the conduct of others that this is standard practice among homeowners.

In all three cases these are expectations people could normally form of individuals in these circumstances, but Sidgwick's implication is that such expectations cannot invariably apply to persons in the relevant circumstances. Thus, the implication is that normal expectations admit of exceptions (I would not be expected to come to the aid of my co-worker if I were already carrying a heavy object). If so, they appear to be similar to Fishkin's ordinary expectations.

David Archard employs the terminology of "general expectations" in his essay, "Moral Partiality." He believes different types of partiality exist and that general expectations are attached to each type. These expectations are shaped by custom, convention, and institutional habit (Archard, 1996, p. 138). The expectations he has in mind are not necessarily moral expectations, but they can take the form of moral expectations. Someone can be morally expected to provide shelter to a family member who has been evicted from his or her apartment if this family member has nowhere else to go. But someone could not be morally expected to do the same for a person to whom he or she is barely acquainted. Hence Archard's general expectations, like the ordinary expectations of Fishkin and the normal expectations of Sidgwick, admit of exceptions. A man who has been evicted from his apartment can expect a family member to provide shelter for him, but someone to whom he is barely acquainted cannot rightly be expected to provide shelter for him. Regarding Archard's account of partiality, I will have more to say momentarily.

To summarize, some writers, following Aristotle's example, speak in terms of what can reasonably be expected of a moral agent. Although what can reasonably be expected of a moral agent is not exactly the same as what can rightly be expected on the agent, the remarks of such philosophers as Lyons, Card, and Williams are helpful in understanding how moral expectation arises as the result of various inter-personal dynamics within society. Other philosophers have characterized moral expectation in ways closely related to reasonable expectation. Fishkin calls attention to courses of action people can ordinarily be expected to undertake, Sidgwick speaks about normal expectations which people form about the behavior of others, and Archard explains how general expectations arise from special types of concern people have for others. An important common denominator among the ordinary expectations of Fishkin, the normal expectations of Sidgwick, and the general expectations of Archard is that their accounts are all designed to accommodate exceptions.

Another recurring theme about moral expectation in the literature is that our moral expectations are frequently shaped or determined by sociological factors. Whether or not we are expected to perform actions which benefit another person depends to a certain extent upon the nature of our relationship to the person. Other things being equal, we are more likely to be expected to act for the benefit of someone to whom we have close ties than someone to whom we do not have close ties. Strangers are people to whom we are least likely to be expected to benefit, especially strangers who are distant. As John Arthur puts it,

"We tend . . . not to expect people to make large sacrifices to distant strangers (Arthur, 1993, p. 852)."

Already we have taken note of Archard's account of general expectations. Another aspect of Archard's account which bears examination, degrees of partiality, is relevant to this section. According to this account, strangers are not treated the same as friends and cannot expect the same special type of concern. Friends, in turn, cannot expect the same special type of concern as a lover or family member. These special types of concern are determined, at least partially, by the closeness of our relationship to a person.

Suppose that you are awakened in the middle of the night by one of your children who has become ill. You recognize that a particular medication is needed for this illness, a medication that you can obtain from a twenty four hour pharmacy. In this scenario you can be morally expected to get up, drive to the pharmacy, and obtain the medication. Judging that your next door neighbor or a friend staying at your house can be expected to do this for your child is much less plausible, even if you are not available to do it. According to Archard's account of partiality, the same type of special concern that can be expected of a family member cannot be expected of a neighbor or friend.

Susan Wolf makes a similar point about how expectations are shaped by considerations of partiality: "For relationships of friendship, and love, not to mention family ties, tend to give rise to special expectations in their participants and frequently put individuals in positions that make them uniquely capable of benefiting and protecting one another (Wolf, 1992, p. 247)." Wolf uses the phrase "special expectations" to make the point that some of the expectations we form about others are special in the sense that their existence is based upon relationships. And she makes specific mention of the relationships of friendship, love, and family ties. We have special expectations of our friends, those we are tied to in a relationship of love, and those related to us by family ties.

Clearly Wolf believes that these are legitimate expectations. We are right to expect more from people to whom we are connected by friendship, love, and family ties than from other people. One basis for this, in Wolf's opinion, is that the people connected to one another in these ways are uniquely capable of benefiting and protecting one another. Those who share ties of friendship, love, or family understand and care for each other better and more deeply than those who do not and hence are in a better position to benefit or protect each other.

But how exactly are these ideas connected? Clearly those who share ties of friendship, love, and family are better able to benefit and protect one another than those who do not. But how does this serve as a basis for saying that we are right to expect more from people to whom we share these ties? Perhaps the idea is that certain kinds of expectations are based upon the fact that these people have an insight into what is best for us in a way that others, or even we ourselves, do not. We can appropriately form expectations of those with such insight in a way that we cannot appropriately form expectations of others. I can rightly expect a family member to be supportive of me in a time of need in part because a family member knows me well enough to know how to be supportive of me. Because a stranger does not know me or know how to benefit me, expecting the same of a stranger is not appropriate.

Marion Smiley speaks about "social expectations" in a discussion of racism and the solution of societal problems connected with racism (Smiley, 1996, p. 23). She believes that one factor governing the appropriateness of the social expectations we form is the community to which we belong. For example, when we form expectations about who should prevent certain types of harm, these expectations depend partly on whether various individuals are considered members of our community. We can more readily expect a member of our own community to work to prevent harm within the community than someone not considered part of our community.

Another factor governing the appropriateness of social expectations discussed by Smiley is the question of who is most effective in solving societal problems. Someone might base his or her expectations upon who can best prevent harm or who can "put her projects aside and do something for someone else (*Ibid.*)." Smiley cites civil rights leader Roger Wilkins as someone who believes that white Americans can be expected to pay more taxes in order to alleviate racism and poverty among persons of color. The expectations Wilkins forms about white Americans are based in part upon the assumption that such taxation is an effective means of solving societal problems connected with racism and poverty. The expectations are also based upon the assumption that the taxation of white Americans is a way to prevent further harm among persons of color.

One writer who has expressed disagreement with Wilkins is Charles Murray. Murray does not believe that white Americans can be expected to pay more taxes to alleviate racism. Smiley notes that part of their disagreement stems from a disagreement about how much white racism has hurt blacks and how much good can be accomplished by government intervention (*Ibid.*). Thus, Murray does not share Wilkins' view that the taxation of white Americans is an effective means of solving societal problems of racism and poverty.

However, the disagreement between Wilkins and Murray also centers around the notion of community. Murray believes that whites should not be "guilt-tripped" into thinking that persons of color are necessarily within their "community of concern." Wilkins, on the other hand, speaks about the "community of Mankind" in the context of discussing who is responsible for whom (*Ibid.*). Both appear to share the view that a member of a community can more readily be expected to work to solve problems within the community than someone not in the community. But, whereas Wilkins sees whites and blacks as members of the same community, Murray does not. Murray believes that whites are not members of the same community of concern. Given this assumption, Murray does not believe that whites can be expected to pay additional taxes to solve societal problems of racism and poverty.

The disagreement between Wilkins and Murray appears to be a paradigm case of what Bernard Barber calls, "conflicting expectations from different social systems." According to Barber, someone's frame of reference with respect to his or her social system will have an impact upon the expectations he or she forms: "Whether we have in mind expectations of the persistence of the moral social order, expectations of technically competent performance, or expectations of fiduciary responsibility, we must always specify the social relationship or social system of reference. . . . Moral communities are often exclusive: 'we' versus 'them' is a common social phenomenon (Barber, 1983, pp. 16–17)." The social expectations described by Smiley are, in Barber's opinion, formed relative to social systems of reference. And people operating within differing social systems of reference may well disagree about expectations or even produce conflicting expectations. The disagreement might even take the form of a "we versus them" mentality. Given that Wilkins and Murray are coming from different social systems of reference, that they disagree about what can be expected of white Americans makes perfect sense according to Barber's model.

Adam Seligman refers to the expectations described by Barber as "role expectations (Seligman, 1997, p. 25)." The notion that expectations people form are formed relative to social systems can be described in terms of roles. When a lifeguard is on duty at a public beach, people form the expectation that he or she will come to the aid of a swimmer in distress. In Barber's terminology, the social systems of our culture give rise to "expectations of technically competent performance" from someone employed as a lifeguard (Barber, 1983, p. 16). In Seligman's terminology, the lifeguard is playing a role defined by the conditions of his or her employment, and on this basis we form role expectations of the lifeguard.

Both Barber and Seligman are concerned with characterizing the concept of trust and drawing connections between trust and expectations. Seligman sees trust as "confidence in the fulfillment of role expectations (*Ibid.*)" (and in the social control and sanctioning mechanisms that ensure such performance). Our trust in the lifeguard is a confidence that he or she will fulfil the role expectations we form. On a more personal level, our trust for our parents is based on a confidence that they will fulfil the role expectations we form about them as parents. When people fail to fulfil these role expectations, we tend to lose confidence, and the undermining of this confidence leads eventually to an erosion of trust.

To summarize, a variety of writers have enunciated views about moral expectations revolving around the theme that the moral expectations we have are shaped by the nature of our relationships with others. General agreement exists that we are more likely to be expected to benefit those to whom we have close ties than those to whom we do not. Archard and Wolf develop this idea by appealing to considerations of partiality. For Archard persons to whom we have a distant relationship cannot expect the same type of concern as those to whom we have a close relationship. Wolf speaks about the "special expectations" which can legitimately be made of us by our family and those with whom we share friendship or love.

Smiley approaches this theme through her account of "social expectations." When confronting the problems of society and the means of solving these problems we form social expectations, and for Smiley these expectations are based on considerations of community and effectiveness. Where people differ in their views of community and effectiveness, as illustrated by Wilkins and Murray, they will differ about the social expectations of various groups of people. Barber believes that social expectations are based upon our frame of reference with respect to a "social system" and that differences about social expectations can be explained in terms of people's having differing frames of reference. Seligman, finally, captures the same idea in his account of "role expectations." The expectations we form about an individual are relative to the social role of the individual. When these expectations are not fulfilled, an undermining of confidence and ultimately an undermining of trust arises.

One theme about moral expectation which commonly surfaces in the literature is that the failure to carry out what we are morally expected to do is a moral failure. In Chapter One I described this moral failure in terms of moral blame. To fail to carry out our moral expectations is always morally blameworthy to at least a modest or minimal degree, and this is true whether or not they are at the same time moral obligations. Others have described this moral failure in somewhat different terms, and in what follows I will consider the views of Lawrence Blum, Robert Audi, and Henry Sidgwick.

In his book, *Friendship, Altruism, and Morality* Blum discusses expectations which have been "raised." When a raised expectation is also a "legitimate" expectation, then in his view there is "some moral defect" if the expectation is not met (Blum, 1982, p. 113). Thus, if a person can legitimately be morally expected to perform an action and the person fails to perform the action, this failure embodies a moral defect of some kind. Blum's view appears to be that the nature of the moral defect depends upon the type of situation. For example, the moral defect is a type of deceit in situations where a person who has made clear that he or she can be relied on or counted on to be kind or helpful does not demonstrate these virtues.

Blum goes on to say that the moral defect which characterizes the failure of moral expectation is less serious that the violation of commitment. If a person makes a commitment to perform an action and does not do so, the failure is a more serious moral defect than if the person fails to perform an act he or she is morally expected but not committed to perform. Perhaps Blum believes that the making of a commitment or promise creates a moral obligation, and hence the person making the commitment is morally required to fulfil the commitment. If this is so, the moral defect is greater than if what is violated is no more than a moral expectation.

Elsewhere Blum describes a continuum of actions "ranging from the noblest acts of selfless altruism to those which can be expected of any decent human being (Blum, 1985, p. 85)." This passage suggests that in Blum's opinion some moral expectations constitute the lowest grade of moral worth or merit when carried out. Some human beings are sufficiently monstrous or depraved that they could not be described as decent human beings, and we would not expect them to carry out these expectations. But everyone who warrants the designation of decent can be expected to perform the actions in this category.

Blum might appear to be implying that people can be exempted from the expectations of morality simply because they are monstrous or depraved. But I believe that Blum's idea here is that some actions can be morally expected of everyone (able to perform them), though some people are so monstrous or depraved that they may lack the ability to perform them. Just as the ought implies can principle states that no one has a moral obligation to do what he or she is incapable of doing, perhaps Blum is relying upon a similar type of principle that no one can be morally expected to do what he or she is incapable of doing. Thus, those who cannot be described as decent human beings are not exempted from these actions because they are not decent. They are exempted because they have, for whatever reason, reached such a state that they simply cannot muster what it takes to perform these actions (in which case they are probably morally responsible for having allowed themselves to reach such a state).

In his book, *Moral Knowledge and Ethical Character*, Audi describes an example in which a happy-go-lucky couple unthinkingly fails to provide for their children's future. If providing for their children's future is something they can be expected to have done, then, according to Audi, their failure to do so is a case of culpably, or at least responsibly, precluding what they ought to have done (Audi, 1997, p. 159). It is not entirely clear what Audi intends by the inclusion of the qualifying phrase, "at least responsibly," but apart from this qualification Audi is saying that the actions of the couple which have precluded their providing for their children's future are actions for which they are culpable. Audi is apparently appealing to a general principle to the effect that we are culpable for the failure to do what we are morally expected to do, or at least the principle that the actions we perform which constitute the failure to do what we are morally expected to do are actions for which we are morally culpable. Thus, what Blum calls a moral "defect" is described by Audi as something for which we are morally culpable.

Sidgwick refers to the failure to carry out our moral expectations as a "disappointment of expectations," a phrase also employed by John Stuart Mill (Mill, 1971, p. 55). When someone forms an expectation that a person will perform an action, the failure of the person to perform the action is a disappointment of the expectation which has been formed. Sidgwick declares that a utilitarian will regard any disappointment of expectations to be *pro tanto* an evil

(Sidgwick, 1981, p. 443). In other words, the utilitarian will judge that any failure to meet a moral expectation will be evil to a certain extent.

Whether Sidgwick wishes to endorse the view of the utilitarian is not clear, but what he says about this view is both intriguing and instructive. He says that the amount of evil generated in the failure to carry out our expectations, at least those generally recognized as normal and reasonable, depends in part upon the, "previous security of the expectant individual." The greater the security or confidence of the expectant individual that the expectation is carried out, the greater the "shock" caused by the subsequent failure to carry it out. And the greater the shock produced, the greater the evil in the subsequent failure to carry it out.

This view should not be taken as embodying a hard and fast rule that a great amount of confidence in the expectation is accompanied by a great amount of evil in the disappointment of the expectation. Sometimes a person can be utterly confident that someone else will carry out a trivial moral expectation, and the resulting evil will be minimal. Instead, the rule Sidgwick articulates should be interpreted as saying that the evil in the disappointment of the expectation tends to be greater in situations where the confidence of the expectant individual is greater, given that the expectation is normal and reasonable to begin with.

Perhaps the underlying idea is that the disappointment experienced by those forming expectations is itself a type of evil. Suppose that I am riding in an automobile driven by a highly respected colleague and our vehicle is pulled over by a police officer. Knowing my colleague well, I form the expectation with great confidence that he will conduct himself with dignity and refrain from saying anything inflammatory to the officer. If to my amazement my colleague begins to utter profanities to the officer, his failure to live up to the expectation is not only an evil but it is a greater evil than if my expectation had not been formed with confidence. The reason for its being greater is perhaps that it creates in me a profound discouragement with my colleague and, in general, a sense of disillusionment with placing trust or confidence in people we consider ourselves to know well. Morally speaking, this type of disillusionment makes the world a worse place, not a better place.

To summarize, several writers have articulated the idea that some type of negative moral status attaches to a person who fails to do what he or she is morally expected to do. Blum believes that when an expectation is raised and the expectation is legitimate, the failure to meet the expectation represents a type of moral defect. The nature of the moral defect, in turn, depends upon the nature of the expectation and the circumstances of the person who fails to fulfil it. Audi believes that a person is culpable for failing to do what he or she is morally expected to do. And Sidgwick speaks about the disappointment of expectations as a type of evil and that, for a utilitarian at least, the evil in the disappointment of expectations increases as the confidence of the expectant individual increases.

I believe that all three views are compatible with the view, presented in Chapter One, that the failure to do what we are morally expected to do is always morally blameworthy. Whether we speak of such a failure as a moral defect, something for which a person is culpable, or as something evil, we can plausibly judge that the person is open to moral blame for this failure. We can plausibly judge that a person who fails to carry out his or her moral expectations is a fitting object of disapproval and hence is deserving of some type of moral censure or blame, at least to a modest or minimal degree. A person cannot simply ignore what can be morally expected of him or her and hope to escape all possibility of moral blame. The person would then be treating moral expectation as a morally neutral concept, and this is not what people mean when they speak of expectation. If anything is clear about the concept of moral expectation, it is that expectation is not a morally neutral concept.

In conclusion, the writers surveyed in this chapter can help us better understand moral expectation by enabling us to see the multiplicity of ways in which expectations are characterized and the reasons for characterizing them in these ways. Expectations can be reasonable, ordinary, normal, or general, depending upon the circumstances. We can observe special expectations, social expectations, conflicting expectations from different social systems, and role expectations. Finally, we can distinguish various ways of characterizing the failure of expectation. The failure can be described as a moral defect, something for which the agent is culpable, or as an evil.

Four

OUGHTS AND EXPECTATIONS

Frequently we learn what is morally expected of us by people telling us what we ought to do. When people tell us about an action we ought to perform or about a course of action we ought to refrain from performing, they are frequently articulating moral expectations about our behavior. If we ought morally to do something, we can reasonably judge that we can be morally expected to do it.

The statement that a moral agent ought to perform an action is sometimes intended to convey the message that the agent has a moral duty or obligation to perform the action. Statements about what we ought to do sometimes function as statements about moral requirements. Perhaps this type of statement is even the paradigm for statements about what people ought to do, at least if "ought" is being employed in a moral sense (clearly non-moral senses of "ought," such as the prudential sense, can be identified and these will fall outside the scope of the present discussion).

One theme of this chapter is that we can distinguish statements where "ought" designates moral duty or obligation from statements in which it designates something moral other than duty or obligation. In recent years some philosophers have argued for a type of moral ought which is weaker than the ought of moral obligation. On this view, to say that someone morally ought to do something is not necessarily to say that he or she has a moral obligation to do it, for a moral ought which does not carry the force of an iron-clad moral requirement is alleged to exist.

My purpose is not to argue that this weaker type of moral ought helps to capture the notion of moral expectation, for acts which we ought to do in this weaker sense form a sub-category of the realm of moral expectation. But to the extent that we can reasonably expect someone to do what he or she ought to do, surveying what some writers have to say about an ought weaker than moral obligation will be instructive. From this we can see that moral expectation is not precisely the same as moral obligation, owing to the fact that the acts captured by the weak ought form a proper subset of the acts that can rightly be expected of us.

Later in this chapter I will discuss the ought implies can principle in the context of the distinction between the ought of moral obligation and a weaker type of ought. My suggestion will be that the version of this principle which applies to the weaker type of ought is defensible, just as is true of the stronger version. I will introduce a principle of fairness in the course of making this point. And I will argue that the fairness principle also applies to moral expectations. On this basis I recommend acceptance of a principle similar to the ought implies can principle which is relevant to moral expectation, the principle that we can be morally expected to perform an action only if we are able to perform the action. In the final section of this chapter I turn to the issue of failing to do what we ought to do. While failing to do what we ought to do is blameworthy, expressing judgments of blame to another who is guilty of such a failure is not always appropriate. I urge that an expression of disappointment is more likely to be appropriate in these contexts, other things being equal, than an expression of blame.

David Little has argued for a distinction between "mandatory oughts" and "permissive oughts." When someone ought to do something in the mandatory sense, then the failure to do it is morally impermissible. The ought of moral obligation clearly falls into the realm of the mandatory ought. When we have a moral duty or obligation to perform an act, then the fact that we ought to perform it is something of a mandatory nature. Permissive oughts, on the other hand, are so named because failing to do what we ought to do in this sense is morally permissible (Little, 1992, p. 169). The failure to do what we permissively ought to do falls short of the failure of moral duty or obligation.

Gift giving can qualify as an example of a permissive ought. Under certain circumstances a person ought to give a gift to another person. But because compelling the giving of gifts does not make sense, the sense of "ought" operative in this context is not the mandatory ought. The sense in which someone ought to give a gift to another is the permissive sense.

Little's example of gift giving can be utilized in the context of moral expectation. Suppose someone receives a formal invitation to a birthday party and subsequently attends the party. We can reasonably judge that the person is expected to bring a birthday gift, and, depending upon the precise circumstances, even morally expected to bring a gift, so that the failure to do so can be at least mildly blameworthy. But to judge that the person has a moral obligation to bring a gift appears mistaken, for someone's being morally required to bring a gift is not in the nature of gift giving. Someone can be morally expected to give a gift, then, even though the person has no moral obligation to do so.

Another philosopher who has argued in favor of a moral ought which is weaker than moral obligation is Claudia Card. In her opinion showing mercy is sometimes something we ought to do in this weaker sense of ought (Card, 1972, p.184). She contends that in some situations we ought morally to show mercy to an offender, even though we have no moral duty or obligation to do so.

Perhaps Card's example can be adapted to the discourse of moral expectation. Cast in the language of moral expectation, her contention would amount to the claim that in some situations we can be morally expected to show mercy without at the same time being morally obligated to show mercy. Suppose that you have lent a small sum of money to a friend with the friend's assurance that the money would be repaid on a particular day. When your friend repays the money one day late and requests mercy on your part, then you can be expected to grant this request.

In "A Defense of Abortion" Judith Jarvis Thomson employs a moral ought weaker than the ought of moral obligation in the context of discussing abortion. In one of her examples involving abortion Thomson argues that if a woman became pregnant as a result of rape, and pregnancy lasted for just one hour, then she ought to allow the fetus the use of her body for that hour (Thomson, 1971, p. 59). To refuse would be indecent. At the same time, she denies any require-ment to do so. We might say, then, that as a consequence of Thomson's view, a woman who has been raped cannot be required to allow the fetus the use of her body, but allowing it to do so could rightly be expected of her if pregnancy lasted just one hour.

In "Famine and Charity" John Whelan argues that situations can be iden-tified in which a moral agent ought to perform an action which he or she is not morally obligated to perform. His explanation of this phenomenon is that no moral requirement that the agent perform this action exists, and no one can justifiably demand that the agent do so; however, the moral agent is still liable for moral criticism for failing to perform the action (Whelan, 1991, p. 151). Thus, the agent's non-performance of the action is morally blameworthy.

The main thrust of Whelan's argument is that giving to charity is some-thing we can be morally expected though not morally required to do. Thus, even though we are not morally required to give to charity, on Whelan's view the failure to give to charity is liable to moral criticism. Perhaps the failure to give to a particular charity on a particular occasion is not something for which we are liable to moral criticism, but the failure to give to charity in general is the failure to do something we morally ought to do. Though the focus of his discus-sion is charity, Whelan provides many examples of a mundane nature. They include holding the door open for someone carrying a large package when it is easily within our power to do so, deciding not to tell a true but embarrassing story we have heard twelfth hand about another person, and expressing grati-tude toward another person who has gone out of his way to do us a favor (*Ibid.*).

Whelan goes on to say that if someone, "fails to do what she ought but is not required to do, then perhaps explanations or apologies will be *expected*, but they will not be demanded (Whelan, 1991, p. 152)." Here Whelan draws an explicit contrast between moral expectations and the moral demands he assigns to the province of moral obligation. Explaining or apologizing for not doing what we ought to do can be expected of us, and presumably it can be morally expected of us, but we have no moral obligation to do so.

The last philosopher I will mention in this section is Julia Driver who, in the context of describing an ought weaker than moral obligation, offers an ex-ample of refusing to donate a kidney to a brother as an act which is morally permissible, though bad (Driver, 1992, p. 287). Her view appears to be that someone ought to donate a kidney to a brother, but not doing so is morally permissible. Although it is something someone ought to do, the failure to donate a kidney is not the failure of moral obligation.

Driver's example can also be described in the language of moral expectation. Here we might say that donating a kidney to a brother is something we can be morally expected to do, even though doing so is not morally obligatory. Declining to donate a kidney to a brother is morally permissible, but at the same time declining to do so is the failure of a moral expectation. Hence declining to do so is morally blameworthy to some degree or other.

These philosophers share the view that moral agents ought to do certain things over and above what they have a moral obligation to do. If the examples they offer are indeed examples of this phenomenon, then they are at the same time examples of what moral agents can rightly be expected but not morally required to do. For, again, judging that we can be morally expected to do whatever we ought morally to do is reasonable. The class of acts these writers have identified, those which are captured by the weak ought, form a subset of the acts which we are morally expected but not morally required to do.

The acts captured by the weak ought form only a portion of the acts which we are morally expected but not morally required to do. But on the basis of the examples these writers have offered, the general conclusion that moral expectation and moral obligation are not identical appears hard to resist. That which we are morally obligated to do will form a proper subset of that which can be morally expected of us, for what we ought to do in the weak sense likewise forms a proper subset of that which can be morally expected of us. In other words, if the realm of moral obligation exhausts the class of moral expectation, no possibility exists of acts which we ought to do in the weak (but not the strong) sense, for these are all acts which we are morally expected to do. But if the writers surveyed here are correct that acts which we ought to do in the weak sense exist, the realm of moral obligation does not exhaust the realm of moral expectation.

In summary, the case for a moral ought weaker than the ought of moral obligation has been presented by Little, Card, Thomson, Whelan, and Driver. Each offers examples of actions we ought morally to perform even though we are not morally required to perform them. These examples include gift giving, showing mercy, giving to charity, expressing gratitude, and apologizing. Under certain circumstances these are all acts we are not morally required to perform but nevertheless we ought to perform. And if we morally ought to perform them, then we can be morally expected to perform them. Thus, the actions described by these writers are actions we can be morally expected to perform.

One reason the acts described by these writers is significant is that the moral life asks us to do more than carry out our moral obligations. If a person believes that everything that we morally ought to do is morally obligatory, then he or she will acknowledge nothing beyond moral obligation which we ought to do. On this view, once we have carried out our moral obligations, we can rest content that we have done everything we ought to do.

But the message of the writers surveyed here is that we ought to do more than is contained in the requirements of morality. With rare exceptions, we are never morally required to give gifts, show mercy, give to charity, express gratitude, or make apologies. These are not the sorts of actions to which moral obligation attaches itself. However, to say that these are never present in the realm of what we morally ought to do appears wrong. To deny that circumstances exist in which we morally ought to perform actions such as these appears to place unnatural limits upon what we morally ought to do.

These writers have made clear that at certain times we ought to perform actions on behalf of other individuals or for the benefit of other individuals even though we are not morally required to do so. And, as Whelan points out, we are liable for criticism if we fail to do so. At times we can rightly be criticized for failing to act for the benefit of others. A man who scrupulously fulfils all of his moral obligations but never makes the slightest effort to act for the benefit of others has not done all that he morally ought to do, and for these failures he is liable for criticism. To fail to do what we ought to do, even in the weak sense of ought, is morally blameworthy to at least some degree.

Having now distinguished the ought of moral obligation from the ought of permissibility, I turn to the ought implies can principle. In simplest terms the principle states that a person ought morally perform an action only if the person is able to perform the action. Conversely, the principle states that if a person is unable to perform an action, the proposition that the person ought to perform it is false. While a few philosophers have raised objections to this principle (Walter Sinnott-Armstrong, Joseph Margolis), it has enjoyed wide appeal among moral philosophers. Most seem to be of the opinion that to judge that a person ought morally to do something that the person is unable to do is unfair.

The ought implies can principle is generally discussed in connection with the ought of moral obligation. Frequently people appeal to this principle to establish that someone is not under a moral obligation to perform a particular action. Because a person cannot perform a particular action, the person is excused from the moral duty or obligation to perform the action. Thus, the non-performance of the action is morally permissible when the action cannot be performed. The principle can also be used to establish that someone can perform an action on the basis of the fact that the person has a moral obligation to do so, but the principle is used far more often as a means for excusing someone from moral obligation.

Can the ought implies can principle be defended when the ought in question is the ought of moral permissibility? We might have some initial hesitation about defending such a principle. When the antecedent of a true material conditional is weakened, a possibility exists that the antecedent no longer serves as a sufficient condition for the truth of the consequent. Though the truth of the proposition "S ought to perform action A" is sufficient for the truth of "S can perform A" when the first proposition refers to the ought of moral obligation, we cannot infer that the same is true when this proposition refers to the ought of moral permissibility.

Nevertheless, the principle is true. To say that someone ought to perform an action in the weak sense of ought still appears to be a sufficient condition for saying that someone is able to perform the action. If judging that someone ought in the strong sense to do something he or she is unable to do is unfair, judging that someone ought in the weak sense to do something which he or she is unable to do is likewise unfair.

Consider the non-performance of an act a person is unable to perform. If we cannot fairly judge that the non-performance is blameworthy as the violation of duty, we cannot fairly judge that the non-performance is blameworthy as the violation of something less forceful than a duty. For if we cannot fairly blame a person at all for failing to perform an act the person is unable to perform, whether the person would otherwise be blamed to a high or low degree scarcely appears to matter. Suppose that a man who is unable to walk is seated in his automobile in a parking lot. Nearby a woman is walking with two small children when a large dog begins to bark viciously and make threatening motions at the children. The woman, seeing the man seated in his automobile and unaware of his inability to walk might ask for his assistance and form the belief that the man ought to walk over and lend assistance.

An application of the ought implies can principle to this scenario yields the verdict that the woman is mistaken in believing that the man ought to walk over and lend assistance. Were she to know of his inability to walk, she would not have formed this belief. Because he cannot walk over and lend assistance, we would be mistaken to say that he ought to walk over and lend assistance. To judge that a man who is unable to perform this action ought to perform it is simply unfair.

The point I wish to make in this example is that nothing appears to turn on whether the woman's belief that the man ought to walk over and lend assistance employs the strong or the weak ought. Suppose for a moment that the man in the automobile were able to walk, that the woman were correct in her belief that he ought to walk over to lend assistance, and that he nevertheless fails to perform this action. Some might argue that in this scenario the man fails to perform an act he is morally obligated to perform, and some might argue that his failure is something less than moral obligation. But regardless of which position is correct, the failure to act is blameworthy only insofar as the man is able to act. The failure of the man to act in the original scenario is not the failure of anything he ought to do in either the weak or strong sense of ought. Hence his failure to act incurs no moral blame.

Earlier the acts captured by the weak ought were said to form a subset of the acts which people are morally expected but not morally required to perform. If the foregoing argument is correct, that the ought implies can principle applies to the weak ought and the strong ought, then the non-performances of the acts comprising this subset incur no blame in situations where the acts cannot be performed. And given this, a person cannot be morally expected to perform such an act if the person is incapable of performing it.

But can a person be rightly expected to perform acts the person is incapable of performing? If the principle employed in the foregoing argument is true, that we cannot fairly blame a person for failing to perform an act the person is unable to perform (henceforth, the "fairness principle"), then no such occasions exist.

For suppose a person is unable to perform a particular action. Then from the fairness principle we can deduce that the non-performance of the act by this person is not the least bit blameworthy. However, one feature of moral expectation discussed earlier is that the failure to do what a person can rightly be expected to do is always blameworthy to at least a minimal degree. Hence the person in question cannot rightly be expected to perform the act. In this way the fairness principle can be used not only to establish that the ought implies can principle applies to propositions employing the weak ought, but it applies to moral expectation in general. A person can never be morally expected to perform an action he or she is unable to perform.

Although this conclusion might seem quite unremarkable, I believe that it is significant. When people form moral expectations concerning others or themselves, they should bear in mind that a moral agent cannot rightly or justifiably be expected to do what he or she is unable to do. Some writers have spoken of justified expectations (Shapiro, 2001, p. 546) or justified sets of expectations (Coleman, 2001, p. 378), and if the fairness principle is true no justified expectations presumably exist with regard to the person and an act he or she cannot perform.

Occasionally this feature of moral expectation appears to be overlooked by people. Sometimes people articulating moral expectations have a tendency to form a callous attitude toward others when these others point out that they are unable to perform the action in question. Those forming the expectations may refuse to believe that this is so, or they might instruct the people claiming the inability to act to simply find a way to perform it.

People who claim an inability to act are not always truthful. Sometimes they feign an inability to act to escape the burden of performing the act, and sometimes they genuinely believe they cannot perform an act they can perform. These situations might convince those forming moral expectations that they should never tolerate excuses and that they should hold firm to their expectations when others claim an inability to act. Obviously, such an attitude is problematic and will lead to people to form false expectations in situations where those who are the object of the moral expectation cannot perform the acts they are expected to perform.

More problematic are people who see no relevance between moral expectation and the inability to act. Those described in the previous two paragraphs need not deny the principle that a person can never be morally expected to perform an act the person is unable to perform. They merely take a skeptical position regarding excuses by people who claim to be unable to perform the relevant actions. But some people seem to reject the principle entirely, adopting the position that the inability to act is no excuse at all for failing to carry out someone's moral expectations. Implicit in this position is also a rejection of the fairness principle; they see nothing unfair in expecting people to do what they are genuinely incapable of doing.

Suppose that a large group of students is conducting a protest. When the police arrive, events begin to spin out of control. The protest turns into a riot, and many students turn to the destruction of property. The leader of the student protest is shocked and appalled by the rioting. The president of the university informs the leader of the protest that he is expected to bring about an end to the rioting at once. The leader of the protest is totally powerless to end the rioting by such a large number of students, and this is obvious to everyone. But the president of the university does not judge that this fact is relevant. All that matters to her is that the leader put an end to the riot immediately.

In this scenario the president of the university is forming an expectation that the leader of the protest perform an action he is incapable of performing. Moreover, she is fully aware that he is incapable of performing the action. She simply does not accept the principle that someone is expected to perform an action only if he or she can perform the action. In addition, she does not accept the fairness principle. She sees nothing unfair in expecting the leader to put an end to the riot when he is in fact incapable of doing so.

Some might argue that the president of the university has formed the expectation only because she is under severe distress and would not do so if she were able to reflect upon the relevant issues in a calm and rational manner. According to this line of argument, anyone who is able to view matters in a calm and rational manner will see the unfairness of expecting a person to perform an action the person is incapable of performing. Someone can form such expectations only in an agitated state of mind.

This thesis, that the fairness principle will invariably be applied to situations by people who examine all of the relevant information in a calm and deliberate manner, does not strike me as self-evident. I am not convinced that a person examining the relevant information in this manner will invariably refrain from forming an expectation that a moral agent perform an action the person knows the agent is unable to perform. Still, I believe that such instances are rare and that most people who reflect on the circumstances will be inclined to view matters in accordance with the fairness principle. And those who regularly or routinely form expectations in violation of the fairness principle will find that the expectations are never carried out.

One principle that does seem self-evident is that a person will never perform an action that the person is incapable of performing. We might succeed in performing an action that we were previously unable to perform, but we will never perform an action we are currently incapable of performing. Hence, when a person is aware that a moral agent is unable to perform an action and nevertheless forms an expectation that the agent perform the action, the person should not be surprised to find that the expectation is not fulfilled. And if the person persists in forming expectations of this type, the person will find that these expectations are never fulfilled. This may not serve to convince the person that such expectations should not be formed, but it might convince the person of the futility of forming them. In the end, offering a decisive proof or demonstration that moral expectation conforms to the fairness principle may be difficult, but someone who doggedly forms expectations in opposition to the principle will experience their futility.

To summarize, the distinction between the strong and weak sense of ought makes possible a distinction between a strong and weak version of the ought implies can principle. I have argued that the fairness principle supports the weak version and the strong version. If someone is incapable of performing an act, judging that he ought to do it is unfair, and this is so regardless of whether the ought in question is intended to be strong or weak. The fairness principle appears to apply as well to those instances of moral expectation which fall outside the realm of what moral agents ought to do. Thus, moral expectation as a whole appears to be governed by the fairness principle. And if this is true, then a person can be morally expected to perform an act only if the person is capable of performing the act.

From the foregoing discussion we may conclude that an agent who ought to perform an action is fully capable of performing the action. In the remainder of this chapter I will address the issue of failing to do what we ought to do. When we fail to do what we ought to do in the strong sense, our failure is a straightforward case of failing to do our duty. But what about cases in which we fail to do what we ought to do in the weak sense? Those who have addressed the distinction between the strong and weak senses of ought have had surprisingly little to say about this matter.

In an earlier chapter I characterized the failure to do what we are morally expected to do as a type of moral failure which is deserving of moral blame, and I believe the same is true of the failure to do what we ought to do in the weak sense of ought. It is a failure less serious that the failure to live up to our moral obligations, but it is nevertheless a type of moral failure deserving of moral blame.

When a moral agent is guilty of this type of moral failure, feelings of shame or remorse are common. The failure to do what we ought to do is deserving of moral blame, but the feelings appropriate to the situation include shame or remorse. Moreover, others often can appropriately express shame for our failure to do what we ought to do. When others tell us that we should be ashamed of ourselves, it is often for failing to do what we ought to have done (in the weak sense of ought). Often they are correct, and we do in fact subsequently feel shame or remorse for the failure.

Another emotion frequently experienced in situations of this type is disappointment. When I fail to live up to what I ought to have done, I can appropriately feel disappointment in myself. When another person fails to live up to what can rightly be expected of him or her, then feeling disappointment in this person's failure is appropriate.

Expressions of disappointment and expressions of blame are not the same. From the fact that a failure to live up to what we ought to do is inevitably morally blameworthy, expressing blame to another for such a failure is not always appropriate. Suppose I ought to express gratitude to another for doing me a favor of considerable magnitude, and I fail to do so. An expression of blame on the part of the person who has done me the favor is perhaps appropriate, but I do not deserve to endure expressions of blame by large numbers of total strangers.

Expressions of disappointment seem to be easier to justify. Suppose that a young boy who has entered a contest wins the chance to interview some prominent baseball players. One player, obviously impatient with the proceedings, refuses to answer any question with more than one or two words. People might understandably feel disappointment in the player's failure to conduct the interview in the way that he arguably ought to do. Moreover, for people, even total strangers, to express their disappointment to the player would not be unseemly.

Naturally, the appropriateness of offering expressions of blame or disappointment varies from situation to situation and depends on factors such as the degree to which the person is blameworthy and the relationship the person bears to the one offering expressions of blame or disappointment. But expressions of disappointment are more likely to be appropriate, other things being equal, than expressions of blame. And someone who offers an expression of disappointment is less likely to be open to charges of judgmentalism than someone who offers an expression of blame.

Five

AGREEMENTS AND EXPECTATIONS

Agreements between two people sometimes proceed in a straightforward manner. Both enter freely and voluntarily into the agreement, both are timely and conscientious in fulfilling the terms of the agreement, and both are satisfied with the outcome and have no regrets about having entered into the agreement. In such agreements expectation plays an obvious role. Each participant forms an expectation that the other will carry out his or her part of the agreement, and each is in fact expected to carry out his or her part of the agreement.

Whether the expectation is moral in nature will depend upon the circumstances. In many standard situations we can be morally expected to carry out our part of the agreement. But if the agreement itself is immoral, we are probably not morally expected to fulfil the terms of the agreement. The same may be true if we are duped or misled regarding the terms of the agreement or about the fulfillment of the agreement by the other party.

In this chapter moral expectation will be discussed in relation to agreements that do not necessarily proceed in a straightforward manner. For purposes of simplicity I restrict the discussion to agreements between two parties. The issues comprising the discussion will be organized by the following categories: (1) The proposal to enter into an agreement, (2) The proposal to dissolve an agreement, (3) The refusal to enter into an agreement, (4) The refusal to dissolve an agreement, and (5) The opposition to the formation or termination of an agreement by a third party.

Within each category I present several situations that serve to illustrate the role of expectation in the dynamics of entering into agreements and dissolving agreements. These situations are by no means exhaustive of the types of situations that can fall under these categories. They are instead selected on the basis of their ability to shed light on the interplay between the formation and alteration of expectations and the formation and termination of agreements between two parties. The types of agreements under consideration will embrace legal and non-legal agreements, formal and informal agreements, and contractual and non-contractual agreements.

The most obvious reason for proposing an agreement is that a person believes the agreement will benefit him or her and that the other party will find the agreement potentially beneficial as well. When parties enter into such agreements, each party forms an expectation that the other will carry out its part of the agreement. Normally the assumption, then, is that these are what some writers call reliable expectations (Coleman, 2001, p. 373). When one person proposes an agreement to another, the person offers to bring about a state of affairs in exchange for the other person's bringing about a different state of affairs. The person to whom the agreement is proposed is justified in forming an expectation that the person is proposing an agreement that is fair, above board, and being offered in good faith.

Sometimes these expectations prove to be false expectations. Suppose that person A proposes an agreement to person B to the effect that A will clear the snow on B's driveway in exchange for fifteen dollars. Person B is in another city and tells A on the telephone that he accepts the terms of the agreement. Here B is justified in expecting that person A is actually going to clear the driveway. Suppose that, unbeknownst to B, his driveway has already been cleared by a snow removal service that happened to have the wrong address for another customer, and A is attempting to capitalize on the situation. In this scenario B's expectation is misplaced because A's proposed agreement is based on deception and therefore not made in good faith. And this is so regardless of whether B ever learns about this deception.

Sometimes people propose agreements to make the best of a situation that does not bode well for them. Imagine that George and his wife live in an apartment building and the inhabitants of the only other apartment in the building are elderly females. After a heavy snowfall George quickly realizes that he is the only inhabitant able-bodied enough to clear the walkway. He knows that the others will expect him to do so, and his wife will inevitably volunteer his services to the others. Before she has a chance to do so, George proposes an agreement to the inhabitants of the other apartment. He offers to remove the snow if they agree to cook dinner for himself and his wife. To George's way of thinking, the agreement will allow him to make the best of an unfortunate situation. The others might question the fairness of this proposed agreement. To them the proposed agreement might have the appearance of a mild form of coercion: George will not clear the driveway unless he receives compensation in the form of a meal. They had been counting on an offer from George's wife and are annoyed that George arrived first with the proposal of an agreement.

Sometimes the proposals of such agreements seem to border on blackmail. Consider an example concerning George's dealings with his neighbor. Over the course of time George learns that his neighbor has a large collection of weapons in a secret room. Some of these weapons are stolen and some are illegal to own. The neighbor has recently begun to anger George by playing loud music in the middle of the night and is unresponsive to George's requests to cease this practice. Thus, George proposes the following agreement: George will continue his silence about the weapons to the law enforcement authorities if the neighbor will cease the practice of playing loud music in the middle of the night.

George's proposed agreement strikes the neighbor as blackmail. The agreement appears to the neighbor as a statement that George will inform the authorities about the weapons collection if he does not get his way about the loud music. Strictly speaking this statement is not entailed by what George actually proposes, for George's proposal leaves open the possibility that he will continue his silence about the weapons no matter what happens. But the neighbor would be foolish to interpret George's proposal any other way. The neighbor has formed an expectation that, though George made no promises, George will keep the secret he so generously shared. From the neighbor's perspective, George violates this expectation in the very proposal of the agreement.

Sometimes the proposal of an agreement constitutes the offering of a bribe. Bribery differs from extortion in at least two ways. While extortion is initiated by the person seeking a payment or favor, bribery is initiated by the person offering a payment or favor. And while extortion involves an element of coercion, the person who is offered a bribe can freely choose to accept or reject the offer.

Suppose George's neighbor comes to realize his folly in telling George about the weapons in his secret room and decides to cultivate George's favor. When George complains about the loud music, he immediately turns the music off. Periodically he brings George bottles of wine, tickets to ball games, and gift certificates to local restaurants. Nothing is said about a connection between these gifts and George's silence. But the neighbor views these gifts as the price of George's keeping silence, and George, delighted to be the recipient, assumes that this is the case. The agreement in this scenario is an unspoken agreement and is accompanied by expectations on both sides. The neighbor forms the expectation that George will continue to keep silent, and George forms the expectation that he will periodically receive gifts of various sorts.

Sometimes an agreement that initially constitutes extortion or blackmail evolves into an agreement which constitutes bribery. Suppose Susan is a successful professional who has pity on a financially strapped family consisting of a single woman with several small children. Every month Susan pays the family's electric bill, and the woman is very grateful for this help. One day an unemployed man moves into the family's house, and Susan, who is a devout Baptist, is scandalized by the new living arrangement. She approaches the woman with the proposed agreement that she will continue paying the family's electric bill if the man moves out.

The woman, who has grown dependent upon the assistance, views this proposed agreement as a form of extortion or blackmail. Clearly Susan will continue the support only if the man is kicked out of the house. The woman immediately agrees with Susan's terms and complies. She continues to have her electric bills paid by Susan. Moreover, to make sure of staying on Susan's good side, she attends Susan's Baptist church from time to time. An unspoken agreement comes into existence. The woman comes to expect that Susan will continue paying her electric bills if she periodically performs actions to cultivate Susan's favor. Susan comes to expect these small bribes on the part of the woman.

All of the cases so far examined involve the proposal of an agreement by one person to another. Next are cases in which one person proposes that an agreement which is in effect be dissolved or terminated. Sometimes person A calls an end to an agreement because person B has not, in A's opinion, carried out his or her part of the agreement in a satisfactory manner. Recall the earlier example in which A proposes to remove the snow on B's driveway in exchange for fifteen dollars. Suppose B learns that a snow removal service has cleared the driveway prior to A's proposing the agreement. Since B entered the agreement with the clear expectation that A clear the driveway, B proposes the dissolution of the agreement and is unwilling to pay fifteen dollars to A. Consequently, A should no longer expect B to pay the fifteen dollars.

People commonly refuse to carry out their side of an agreement when they perceive that the other party has not adequately done what it agreed to do. Sometimes situations of this type result from a misunderstanding: One party genuinely believes it is carrying out its part of an agreement, while the other party holds an expectation of something quite different. In other situations one party simply forgets to carry out its part of an agreement, and the other party understandably exhibits reluctance to do what it has agreed to do.

Occasionally one person proposes to dissolve an agreement with no clear time-span when events take place that seem to render the agreement obsolete. A man who for years has hired a neighbor to mow his lawn proposes to dissolve the agreement when a granddaughter expresses interest in having the work. The neighbor might have expectations that the man will indefinitely continue to pay for his services. But the granddaughter, aware of the previous arrangement, forms an expectation that her employment has a higher priority in the eyes of her grandparent than that of the neighbor.

In other cases a person may propose to dissolve an agreement because the need for the agreement no longer exists. Two people reach an agreement that they will telephone each other long distance once a week on an alternating basis. When one of them moves to the same city as the other, the weekly long distance calls are unnecessary. Sometimes a person might propose dissolving an agreement when forces outside his or her control make carrying out the terms of an agreement impossible. If someone's part of an agreement is to perform certain tasks and the person sustains an injury that makes the performance of these tasks impossible, he or she has good reason to propose that the agreement be dissolved.

These cases require those who have entered into these agreements to adjust their expectations to changing circumstances. When one party is approached by the other with a proposal to dissolve an agreement and the proposal strikes the first party as based upon legitimate reasons, he or she will likely no longer expect the other to fulfil the terms of the agreement. In cases where the parties disagree on whether they have legitimate reasons to dissolve the agreement, the situation is more complex and the adjustment of expectations will depend upon the interplay between various factors.

The proposal to dissolve an agreement may be based upon the realization that the agreement is flawed to begin with. The realization that carrying out the terms of an agreement will cause harm to the parties involved or others is a reason to propose dissolving it. The realization that carrying out the terms of an agreement involves illegal or immoral activity is likewise a reason to propose dissolving it. The parties may disagree on whether to proceed with dissolving the agreement. But whether they agree or disagree, an adjustment of expectations is almost surely necessary. The party proposing to dissolve the agreement is most unlikely to carry out his or her part of the agreement after having arrived at realizations of this type.

People might propose to dissolve an agreement, finally, for the simple reason that they are no longer willing to carry out their part of the agreement. Perhaps they discover that carrying out their part of the agreement is highly demanding and involves unforeseen sacrifices. If neither party has yet fulfilled its part of the agreement, the two parties might agree to dissolve the old agreement. If, on the other hand, one party has already carried out its part of the agreement, the idea of dissolving the agreement is likely to be distasteful. Indeed, the whole point of forming an agreement in the first place is to prevent this very state of affairs from occurring. If a person's expectation that the other party carry out its part of the agreement is not met in such cases, the person is justified in finding the situation unfair.

I turn next to situations in which people refuse to enter into agreements. Some obvious reasons why people might decline the offer of entering into an agreement are as follows. First, they might believe that the other party is requesting too much. Second, they might believe that the other party is offering too little. Third, they might believe the other party is incapable of doing what it proposes to do. Fourth, they might believe themselves incapable of doing what is requested. Fifth, they might believe that the other party is not to be trusted to carry out its part of the agreement.

Another interesting reason for people to refuse entering into an agreement is that they believe the other party should carry out what it proposes to do regardless of any agreement. Suppose that you are hosting a lavish garden party and two total strangers materialize and begin helping themselves to food and beverages from the buffet. When you approach them and ask them to leave, one of them proposes an agreement: If you permit them to make a brief sales presentation, they will leave immediately afterward. Such an agreement would strike you as bordering on the preposterous.

Another example of this phenomenon involves two college roommates. One hangs a poster that contains racist slogans. The other is offended by these slogans and would be ashamed to have her friends and family members see the poster. She asks her roommate to take the poster down. The roommate responds by proposing that she will do so if the other will agree not to leave her possessions scattered all over the floor.

The roommate offended by the poster finds the proposal of this agreement repugnant. In her opinion, the racist poster should not be hung in someone's room, and its removal should not be part of an agreement requiring someone to fulfil various conditions. Thus, she believes her roommate is expected to take down the poster, and the fulfillment of this expectation should not be contingent on the fulfillment of her roommate's expectations.

Another reason why people might decline the offer of entering into an agreement is that they find the agreement unfair to the person proposing it. Suppose that a man in a tavern who is heavily intoxicated tells you that he is in no shape to drive home, a statement with which you readily agree. He then requests that you drive him home. His money is gone, but he offers his high school class ring as payment for driving him home.

I believe few people would find this offer attractive. The problem with the proposed agreement is not that the ring is something few people would desire to own. The problem is that the man is offering to part with a valuable possession in exchange for a trivial favor, and the offer is one he is unlikely to consider in a sober state of mind. For this reason you can be expected to decline the offer.

The refusal to enter into an agreement, finally, might be based upon the belief that you yourself are not to be trusted in carrying out the terms of the agreement. You might believe of yourself that, despite good initial intentions, you are likely to leave your part of the agreement incomplete. Imagine that a friend proposes an agreement according to which you and the friend each jog at least ten miles per week. You know this friend well, and you have little doubt that the friend will be conscientious in carrying out her part of the agreement. But you also know yourself well and know that you lack the self-discipline to carry through the agreement beyond the initial few weeks. You do not wish your friend to form expectations that you will carry through the agreement indefinitely, and in the end you decline to enter into the agreement.

Next I turn to situations in which one party refuses to dissolve an agreement when the other party proposes to do so. Here we must bear in mind that an agreement is in effect, and hence each party expects the other to carry out its part of the agreement. We must also bear in mind that an agreement can be dissolved without securing the agreement of the other party. In many types of situations one party can simply break the agreement by refusing to carry out its part of the agreement. An example would be one party's breaking off the engagement of marriage without securing the agreement of the other party.

But in many cases securing the agreement of the other party to dissolve an old agreement is advantageous, for breaking an agreement unilaterally can damage a person's credibility. Suppose, then, that one party wishes to dissolve an agreement and also wishes the other party to agree to dissolve it. Why might the other party refuse to dissolve the agreement?

One reason why a person might refuse to dissolve an agreement is that the person knows that the agreement is beneficial to him or her. For example, suppose that John rents an apartment for five hundred dollars per month. John and his landlady reach an agreement that John will promise to pay the rent for ten years in exchange for her assurance that the rent will remain the same for ten years. After one year John sublets the apartment to someone willing to pay John eight hundred dollars per month. John continues to pay the landlady five hundred dollars per month, and he pockets the difference. The landlady learns about this arrangement and believes it is unfair. Her expectation that John himself occupy the apartment has not been fulfilled. Thus, she proposes to dissolve the old agreement, and John, not surprisingly, refuses to do so.

Another reason why people might refuse to dissolve an agreement is to prevent the other party from securing something more beneficial. Suppose that in the previous example it is the landlady who finds someone willing to pay her eight hundred dollars per month for the apartment. She attempts to dissolve the agreement she has reached with John in order to rent the apartment to the other person. Naturally, John refuses to dissolve the agreement. John could easily find another apartment for five hundred dollars, but his expectation is that the landlady stand by the agreement.

Sometimes situations of this type occur in professional sports. An athlete signs a multi-year contract and becomes the highest paid player in his or her sport. A couple of years later another athlete signs a contract and becomes the highest paid player in that sport. The first athlete becomes agitated and demands a new contract with more money. The owner of the team now must decide whether to agree to dissolve the old contract and draw up a new contract.

Another reason why a person might refuse to dissolve an agreement is that the person believes that agreements have an integrity of their own and should not be dissolved without reasons of the most compelling kind. Such a belief is bound up with expectations that each party fulfils its part of the agreement unless compelling reasons can be found to alter these expectations. If one party wishes to dissolve an agreement, then, on this view, the other party should be resistant and demand that the other's reasons are suitably compelling. This type of resistance is potentially beneficial in setting a good example to others about the integrity of agreements and the importance of honoring an agreement into which one has entered.

We might refuse to dissolve an agreement simply because we have already carried out our side of the agreement and the other party has not. The other party may be, in effect, asking to be released from carrying out its side of the agreement. Here our expectations that the other party fulfil its part of the agreement may be even more intense than when the agreement was initiated. If the other party is unable to do what it agreed to do or does not care whether we approve the termination of the agreement, then we might as well resign ourselves to dissolving the agreement. But in general we will continue to expect that the terms be carried out as originally agreed, and this expectation will form the basis for refusing to dissolve the agreement.

Sometimes the refusal to dissolve an agreement may result from the belief that continuing the agreement is in the best interests of the other party. Recall the example in which Susan pays the electric bills of the woman with the small children. Suppose that friends of the woman learn about this arrangement and encourage her to dissolve the arrangement on the grounds that accepting free handouts is undignified and will damage her self-esteem. The friends are not proposing an alternative source of income; they are only insisting that she find a way to pay her own electric bills. When the woman informs Susan that she wishes to dissolve the agreement, Susan is astonished and manages to dissuade the woman from following the bad advice of her friends. In the end the woman continues to expect the assistance with her monthly electric bills. Her proposal to dissolve the agreement has been successfully countered by Susan's refusal to dissolve the agreement.

Up to this point the discussion has been limited to dealings between the two parties who have formed an agreement or are considering the formation of an agreement. Now let us expand the discussion to consider third parties who are affected by the presence or absence of such agreements. Sometimes third parties have a vested interest in having two parties reach an agreement, for some agreements are beneficial not only to the parties reaching the agreement but to others as well.

A prospective bride and her parents negotiate with one another on where their upscale wedding reception will be held. When they eventually reach an agreement to hold it at a particular reception hall, the owner of the establishment is one beneficiary of the agreement. The bride forms the expectation that her parents will honor the agreement to host the reception at this location, and the parents form an expectation that their daughter will not change her mind and begin to insist on alternative arrangements. The owner of the reception hall is not in a position to expect that they will choose her place of business. But once they book a date and select a dinner menu, she expects that they will fully live up to the terms of the agreement, and provide suitable gratuities to her staff.

In this section I focus upon situations in which a third party is opposed to the formation of an agreement and situations where a third party is opposed to the termination of an agreement. A third party's opposition to the formation of an agreement may be rooted in the belief that it was unfairly excluded from the process of entering into the agreement.

Sometimes a third party's belief that it has been unfairly excluded from an agreement is justified. Imagine that you and a friend with no money are vacationing together in your automobile. You have set a fairly rigorous itinerary for the trip, and on a day with a particularly long drive scheduled your friend announces that he has promised a ride to someone he has just met. This person would like to be driven to her home, and doing so will require two to three additional hours of driving to accommodate her wishes. Her expectation is that she will be driven home; after all, this is what she has just been promised. Your friend expects the same, for he believes that promises should always be honored. You, on the other hand, feel that you have been unfairly excluded from the agreement, and your expectation is that the others view the situation from your perspective and be willing to dissolve their agreement.

In some situations a third party's belief that it has been excluded from an agreement is not clearly justified. The owner of a tavern finds that a customer has left behind a brand new leather jacket. After no one claims it for a couple of months, the owner begins to wear it on an occasional basis. A customer offers him one hundred dollars for the jacket, and the owner agrees to sell it. The person who left the jacket behind eventually returns from an extended vacation to claim his jacket and is dismayed to learn about the agreement reached in his absence. He expects the customer with the jacket return it at once, but neither party to the agreement is persuaded that this expectation is justified.

Another reason a third party may oppose an agreement is that the agreement is harmful to the interests of a fourth party. A young man, desperate for money, forms an agreement with a friend to sell several expensive pieces of his mother's jewelry. A neighbor overhears the conversation between the young man and his friend. She tells the young man that he will do no such thing, and she immediately telephones his mother at her place of employment. The agreement between the young man and his friend is not harmful to the neighbor, but she is nevertheless motivated to intervene on behalf of the mother. Her expectation is that the young man should sell nothing belonging to his mother without the mother's knowledge or permission.

An agreement might be opposed by a third party that becomes aware that the agreement is unfair to one of the parties entering into the agreement. If a person witnesses an agreement which involves taking unfair advantage of a child or an elderly person suffering from dementia, the person might well protest the agreement and make an effort to have the parties nullify it. People can be expected to refrain from preying upon such individuals, and this fact can motivate a third party to intervene.

A third party might also intervene on behalf of someone whose ignorance of certain information puts him or her at a severe disadvantage. At a garage sale a dealer in antiques recognizes several valuable pieces marked with price tags of a dollar each. Clearly the person selling these items is unaware of their true value. When a competing dealer in antiques snaps them up, the first dealer quickly informs the seller that the pieces are worth several hundred times the marked price. The second dealer is angry about the interference of the first dealer, for he holds that a customer has a right to have the pieces for the asking price. But the first dealer holds an expectation that a dealer not take advantage of someone in a state of ignorance about the value of the pieces.

A third party may even intervene on behalf of both parties to prevent an agreement that is potentially harmful to them. When two teenagers who are heavily intoxicated form an agreement to perform dangerous stunts on the roof of a tall building, a friend might attempt to dissuade them. The friend opposes the agreement because he worries about the possibility of their suffering serious injury. Each of them forms an expectation that the other join in performing the stunts, but the friend forms an expectation that they not engage in such dangerous and reckless behavior.

All of these situations involve a third party standing in opposition to the formation of an agreement. Situations in which a third party opposes the termination of an agreement will now be considered. Imagine that an agreement is in place between two parties, and these parties are now seriously considering terminating this agreement. Reasons why a third party might oppose their doing so will now be considered.

Obviously, a third party will be inclined to oppose the termination of an agreement that is beneficial to its own interests. In a small town two mechanics compete for the local business. They reach an agreement to do free repair work for the inhabitants of the town who are too poor to afford the repair work. For several years this agreement is in effect. During this time each mechanic expects the other to be doing free repair work for poor people, and some of these people come to expect this benefit. When a third mechanic sets up shop in the same town and does no free repair work, the two who have formed the agreement are quietly tempted to dissolve their agreement. One senior citizen who has been the beneficiary of free repairs for several years learns that they are considering the termination of the agreement and encourages each of them to re-consider.

A third party may wish to oppose the termination of an agreement which, although it is not particularly beneficial to its interests, serves to prevent a state of affairs which is detrimental to its interests. Two brothers jointly inherit a vacant parcel of land from their late father's estate. A developer desires to purchase the land and turn it into a mobile home community, and the developer offers the brothers a large sum of money for the land. The brothers are astonished by the size of the offer, but they agree not to sell on the grounds that such a community would spoil the appearance of the area.

When the developer approaches them six months later with a significantly higher offer, they are greatly tempted to abandon their earlier agreement. A neighbor living adjacent to the parcel of land is aware of the brothers' agreement not to sell and learns about the subsequent possibility that they will terminate the agreement. The neighbor knows that the presence of a mobile home community will have a devastating impact upon the value of his property. His expectation is that the brothers stick to their original agreement, and he urges them to do so.

Another reason for a third party to oppose the termination of an agreement is that a fourth party stands to be adversely affected if the agreement is no longer in place. Here the underlying issues may be the same as in cases of a third party's opposing the formation of an agreement: the protection of those unable to protect themselves or those not present to protect themselves, intervention on behalf of those whose ignorance of the situation places them at a disadvantage, and so forth. In each of these situations an agreement protects the interests of such parties, and intervention is required to keep the other parties from exploiting them by removing that agreement.

Finally, a third party's motivation for opposing the termination of an agreement is that the third party has a respect for the integrity of an agreement. Suppose that two sisters form an agreement to take turns running errands once a week for their grandmother. They know that their grandmother has difficulty getting out, and they form the agreement because they want to be of assistance to her. Unfortunately, after several months they grow weary of these errands, and they discuss the idea of terminating the agreement. They are busy with schoolwork and an assortment of other activities, and they feel that they can easily justify this idea to their grandmother.

Their mother is strongly opposed to the termination of their agreement. She is worried about the effect it will have on the grandmother, but her main reason for opposing her daughters' termination of the agreement is that she wants her children to learn to honor commitments. She does not want her children growing up with the idea that agreements should be honored when convenient and that they can be cast aside when people grow weary of them. She has an expectation that her children appreciate and respect the integrity of agreements, and she expects that they will not cast aside agreements when they no longer feel like carrying out the terms of the agreement.

In this chapter expectation has been viewed in relation to agreements or prospective agreements between two parties. When two parties form an agreement, the role of expectation is typically clear and straightforward: each party is expected by the other party to carry out its part of the agreement. I hope to have shown that many complexities can enter into the process of forming and dissolving agreements, and the role of expectation takes on complications and complexities accordingly.

The purpose of this discussion has not been to draw up an exhaustive list of reasons for proposing to enter an agreement, proposing to dissolve an agreement, refusing to enter an agreement, refusing to dissolve an agreement, and opposing the formation or termination of agreements between other parties. Within each of these categories I have highlighted reasons whose relation to the formation of expectations is of interest. In some cases I have made explicit mention of the expectations attendant to the agreements under consideration, and in other cases I have judged that the expectations of the parties concerned were sufficiently obvious that pointing them out is unnecessary.

To summarize, when someone proposes to enter into an agreement, the other party is justified in having an expectation that the agreement is fair. However, sometimes the agreement that is proposed qualifies as a form of coercion or even blackmail, and sometimes it qualifies as a form of bribery. The proposal to dissolve an argument can be the result of one party's perception that the other party has not carried out its part of the agreement, at least not in a satisfactory manner. This may be due to a misunderstanding, forgetfulness, or uncertainty about the time-span of the agreement. Sometimes the proposal to dissolve an agreement results from a realization that circumstances have rendered it obsolete, that the agreement is flawed in the first place, or that someone is simply unwilling to carry out his or her part of the agreement. These situations require the parties to the agreement to be ready to adjust their expectations.

The refusal to enter into an agreement can be the result of a perception that the terms are unfavorable or that one party is incapable of, or not to be trusted with, carrying out its part of the agreement. In addition, one party might believe that the other party should do what it proposes to do regardless of an agreement being reached. And the refusal to enter into an agreement could be based upon a belief that the agreement is unfair to the very party proposing it. The refusal to dissolve an agreement can result from a reluctance to terminate an agreement beneficial to oneself or a reluctance to allow the other party to enter into a different agreement more favorable to its interests. It can also result from a conviction that agreements possess an inherent integrity, a realization that only one party has carried out what it agreed to do, and a conviction that the termination of the agreement is not in the best interests of the other party.

A third party can be motivated to stand in opposition to an agreement because it feels that it has been unfairly excluded from the agreement, because it feels that the agreement is unfair to a fourth party, or because it feels that the agreement is unfair to the parties who have formed the agreement. A third party can be motivated to oppose the termination of an agreement which either benefits its own interests or prevents something detrimental to its interests. In addition, a third party can oppose the termination of an agreement because of its concern to protect the interests of a fourth party or out of its concern for the inherent sanctity of agreements.

Six

AVOIDING EXPECTATION

Moral expectation is not typically something people welcome. Learning that we have a moral expectation to perform a particular act is like learning that our employer has suggested an additional task to perform before leaving for home. We are unlikely to be pleased or joyous in receiving this news. People do create moral expectations for themselves, as when they make promises or volunteer for certain activities. But in these cases people are usually selecting actions they do not mind performing. When people learn that expectations not of their own choosing have been placed on them, the situation is different. Frequently they are being asked to do something they aren't inclined to do, and sometimes they are being asked to do something they are strongly inclined not to do.

That people sometimes seek to avoid moral expectation is not surprising. One way to deal with unwanted or unwelcome expectations, naturally, is to ignore them. The problem with this approach to avoiding moral expectation is that we incur moral blame. While some moral agents may not be bothered with the idea that they are incurring blame through the avoidance of expectation, I believe that many other moral agents are conscientious enough about the moral life that they will seek alternative solutions when seeking to avoid moral expectation. Ignoring moral expectation is not the only way of avoiding moral expectation.

Two ways of avoiding moral expectation can be distinguished. First, we can avoid moral expectation by escaping from it. Here we are confronted with a moral expectation and we find a way to detach the moral expectation from applying to ourselves. The expectation has not gone out of existence, but it has been altered so that it no longer attaches to the person in question, at least not in its present form. Second, we can avoid moral expectation by eliminating or dissolving it. Here we are confronted with a moral expectation and we find a way to make it disappear. The expectation goes out of existence, and we no longer have any reason to be concerned with it. Alternatively, we can eliminate the possibility of an expectation by causing an expectation that would otherwise attach to us never to have a chance of coming into existence.

The first portion of this chapter is devoted to a discussion of escaping from moral expectation. The second portion is devoted to a discussion of eliminating moral expectation, including eliminating the possibility of moral expectation. The final section deals with the partial avoidance of moral expectation. In this section a distinction is introduced between the bare fulfillment of an expectation and a more robust fulfillment in which a person goes beyond the minimal of what is necessary to fulfil it.

When someone escapes from a moral expectation, the escape can be either temporary or permanent. Suppose person A is expected to help person B by performing a task on a particular day. Person A subsequently has an opportunity to travel with friends on a trip during which they plan to be out of town on the day in question. Person B graciously encourages person A to travel, and they postpone the time when A performs the task. The expectation that A perform the task has not been eliminated, but it is slightly altered in such a way that A can temporarily avoid carrying it out. In such cases the expectation is probably not what some have called a settled expectation (Shapiro, 2001, p. 539).

The permanent escape from a moral expectation can take a variety of forms. Sometimes the temporary avoidance of a moral expectation can turn into a permanent avoidance. In the previous example person A returns from travelling with friends, and persons A and B both forget to re-schedule A's performing the task on B's behalf. It is not a particularly high priority for either of them. In the end, person A never does fulfil the expectation. The expectation does not go out of existence, but A manages to avoid it on what turns out to be a permanent basis.

One way to escape a moral expectation on a permanent basis is to cause the expectation to apply or attach to another moral agent. Recall the example in the opening chapter in which a woman, her arms clutching packages, is standing in the rain struggling to open the door. You are standing next to the door, and a moral expectation to open the door attaches to you. Now alter the example so that you take steps to avoid the expectation. When you see the woman approaching with an armful of packages you quickly move to another part of the store, because you anticipate that the expectation will otherwise attach to you. After you move away from the door, the expectation comes to attach itself to someone else in the general vicinity of the door.

This example is a bit unrealistic, for people do not normally take pains to escape from an expectation that can be satisfied with such minimal effort. Perhaps more realistic is an example in which an automobile which is out of control causes grave injury to several pedestrians before crashing into a utility pole. Anticipating that some type of unpleasant moral expectation will attach to those present at the scene of the accident, you flee the scene. In this way you manage to avoid a moral expectation that now attaches to the other bystanders present at the scene.

Naturally, those who flee from moral expectation in ways similar to these can incur moral blame. When people are in a position to lend assistance to others and make efforts to avoid the expectation to lend assistance, these efforts are themselves capable of qualifying as morally blameworthy. Just as we are blameworthy for failing to carry out a moral expectation, we can be blameworthy for fleeing from an opportunity to assist others in need. At the very least, it is behavior that warrants shame. To be observed engaging in this sort of behavior would be shameful.

Perhaps some moral expectations are actually second level or meta-level expectations. If someone can be morally expected to refrain from avoiding a particular moral expectation, as appears reasonable, then the expectation to re-frain is an expectation about an expectation. We satisfy the meta-level expecta-tion by ensuring that the expectation within its scope attaches to us. Thus, de-pending upon the circumstances, we might judge that a person at the scene of an accident can be morally expected to remain there and ascertain whether he or she can be of assistance.

Sometimes escaping from a moral expectation is a simple matter of re-questing that someone else fulfil the expectation. If someone has previously agreed to perform a task and becomes ill when the time comes to perform it, he or she may make arrangements for someone else to step in and perform the task. The expectation then attaches to the person who agrees to perform the task in place of the person who is ill.

Someone might object that the expectation that attaches to the second person is no longer the same as that which attaches to the person who becomes ill. According to this point of view, the expectation attaching to the ill person goes out of existence and an entirely new expectation attaches to the second person as soon as this person agrees to serve as a substitute. I do not propose to take a definite stand regarding the criteria of identity for expectations, and I concede that the point of view reflected in this objection may be correct. If it is correct, then the distinction offered earlier between escaping expectations and eliminating expectations stands in need of revision. The revision can consist in broadening the criterion of escaping an expectation to include cases where one expectation goes out of existence and another virtually identical expectation attaching to another moral agent comes into existence. The details are not cru-cial to the discussion at hand, as long as we acknowledge the basic distinction between escaping from an expectation and eliminating an expectation.

Another way of escaping a moral expectation is by performing actions that fulfill a different expectation. Suppose one brother is expected to weed one patch of garden and the other brother is expected to weed another. The tasks are of comparable duration and difficulty. One brother is confused about who is assigned to which patch and proceeds to weed the wrong patch. Under the cir-cumstances, the other brother can reasonably consider himself to be expected to weed the other patch. The other brother cannot reasonably consider himself to have accomplished his share of the weeding. And the brother who weeds the wrong patch can consider himself to have escaped the expectation to weed the patch originally assigned to him. He escapes one expectation by fulfilling an-other, and the expectation he escapes now attaches to his brother.

When the expectation to refrain from an action attaches to a person the possibility of escape also exists. Several friends regularly enjoy each others' company at a local tavern. They travel together in one vehicle, take turns driv-ing, and on each occasion the driver of the vehicle is expected to refrain from partaking of alcoholic beverages for the evening. One evening the driver for the occasion notices that one friend is drinking non-alcoholic beverages, and the driver requests this friend to serve as the substitute driver for the return trip. When the friend agrees to this proposal, the driver is no longer expected to refrain from alcoholic beverages. In this way the driver comes to escape from the expectation to refrain.

An agent can escape from a moral expectation without even desiring to escape. Suppose that I agree to perform a task. Someone else judges that I lack the expertise to perform the task properly and informs me that he is going to perform it instead. Reluctantly, I step aside and agree that he will be the one to perform the task. Here I am no longer expected to perform the task, and it is he who is now expected to perform it. Without desiring to escape the moral expectation to perform the task, this is what in fact takes place.

An agent can escape from a moral expectation without being aware of escaping the expectation. Suppose that I volunteer to perform a task. The person to whom I volunteer accepts my offer but later comes to doubt my ability to perform the task properly. Without my realizing it, this person contacts others and has the task performed by someone else. As soon as someone else agrees to perform the task, I am no longer expected to perform it. Thus, I escape the expectation to perform the task without being aware that this is so.

To summarize, we can avoid moral expectation by escaping from it or by eliminating it. When we escape from an expectation, the expectation no longer attaches to us in its present form, and the escape can be either temporary or permanent. One way to escape permanently from an expectation is to cause an expectation that would otherwise attach to ourselves to attach to someone else. Such behavior, however, may constitute the violation of a meta-level expectation. Other ways of escaping from moral expectation include persuading someone else to perform actions on our behalf that satisfy the expectation and fulfilling a different but closely related expectation. Sometimes we can escape an expectation to refrain from a particular course of action. Finally, we can escape from a moral expectation without desiring to escape or without knowing that we have done so.

The elimination of a moral expectation occurs when we avoid a moral expectation by the expectation's ceasing to exist (subject to the possible qualification discussed previously) or by eliminating the possibility of its coming into existence. One way of eliminating a moral expectation is by fulfilling the expectation. Presumably, a moral expectation that has been successfully fulfilled is no longer present, and people sometimes desire simply to get the expectation out of the way by fulfilling it at once. But the ensuing discussion will concentrate on the elimination of an expectation in the interests of being spared from dealing with it.

Those of a Meinongian persuasion might object to equating the elimination of an expectation with its going out of existence. On such a view an expectation need not attach to a moral agent in order to exist, and hence the elimination of an expectation is nothing more than detaching the expectation from a moral agent. Although the idea of a vast number of unattached expectations appears dubious, I will acknowledge that this is one possible view of the matter, and nothing of substance in the ensuing discussion will presuppose its falsity.

Sometimes a moral expectation can be eliminated by our being excused from fulfilling it. If we have agreed to bring about a state of affairs, then we can be expected to do so. But if we persuade the person with whom we have an agreement to excuse us from it, we can, depending upon the particular circumstances, cause the expectation to be eliminated. Moreover, if we subsequently become incapacitated and cannot perform the requisite actions, we are excused from doing so. Even if the person with whom we have an agreement does not judge that we ought to be excused, the expectation is in fact eliminated (or, if someone else steps in to perform the requisite actions, we escape from the expectation). As discussed earlier, we cannot be expected to do what we are incapable of doing.

One way to avoid a moral expectation is to remove ourselves from the vicinity where we would otherwise acquire a moral expectation. In an earlier example someone flees the scene of a traffic accident to avoid whatever unpleasant expectation are thereby created, and the expectations attach to the other bystanders. But if no other bystanders are present, then no possibility exists of a moral expectation attaching to a bystander. In this type of example the agent does not eliminate a moral expectation as such. Instead, the agent avoids moral expectation by eliminating the possibility of acquiring an expectation.

This manner of avoiding moral expectation can occur in ways other than removing oneself from a particular vicinity. Suppose that an in-law with a disagreeable personality telephones periodically with requests for a meal or a loan, and he never calls for any other reason. You are not necessarily expected to grant his requests. But you are expected to treat him in a civil manner, and you are expected to provide reasonable excuses if you elect to turn down his requests. If you have a telephone with caller identification, you can avoid these expectations by declining to lift the receiver when the telephone rings and identifies him as the caller. You are thereby eliminating the possibility of acquiring these expectations.

Behavior of this type is common. When people don't feel like dealing with expectations, they frequently take steps to avoid the expectations before they materialize. As before, this is not exemplary behavior, and it often qualifies as blameworthy. But perhaps people assume that eliminating the possibility of an unpleasant expectation is less blameworthy than allowing it to materialize and then failing to satisfy it. In any case, they may be violating a different expectation in the effort to avoid an expectation. A case could be made that someone is expected to answer the telephone when he or she knows that a family member is calling for assistance, as opposed to a tele-marketing representative attempting to make a sale.

A more pro-active approach to eliminating moral expectation is to bring about alterations in our environment that cause the elimination of the expectation. An extreme example of this phenomenon is to poison a cat to avoid the inconvenience of feeding it every day. The expectation that we feed the cat every day is obviously eliminated when the cat is no longer alive. Of course, we are violating a different expectation, for we surely can be expected to refrain from killing the cat for such a frivolous reason. But we nevertheless successfully eliminate the expectation to feed it every day. The elimination of the cat causes the elimination of the expectation to feed it every day.

Fortunately, less drastic methods of eliminating expectations exist. Suppose that a parent grows weary of the expectation of monitoring her son's use of the family computer. This expectation can be eliminated by destroying the computer, but it can be eliminated in other ways as well. The computer can simply be locked in a closet or cabinet. If the monitoring is necessary because of the son's use of the internet, the parent can remove the modem, assuming it is external, and prevent him from using the internet. Clearly, in a variety of ways she can eliminate the expectation to monitor her son's use of the computer.

The expectation to refrain from behavior of a particular sort can also be eliminated by altering our environment. Suppose that a tray of cupcakes is setting on the kitchen counter, and you are expected to refrain from eating them. The cupcakes are destined to be included in a church auction to raise money for charity. If the expectation to refrain becomes too difficult to resist, you might resort to such extreme measures as destroying them or distributing them to neighbors. When the cupcakes are no longer in existence, neither is the expectation to refrain from eating them. Ironically, the same is true if you consume them. By eating all of the cupcakes you simultaneously rid yourself of the expectation to refrain from eating them.

Bringing about no one's holding an expectation is not sufficient to eliminate a moral expectation. As argued in Chapter Two, someone's holding an expectation that an agent perform an action is neither necessary nor sufficient for the agent to be expected to perform the action. Hence the elimination of an expectation requires more than people's no longer holding the expectation. If someone is expected to perform an action and over time everyone forgets that this is the case, then the person may escape criticism or censure for failing to fulfil the expectation. But this does not mean that the expectation is eliminated; nor does it mean that the person escapes moral blame by failing to fulfil it.

In special cases the expectation is eliminated when someone holding the expectation gives it up. If someone has owed you five dollars for a considerable length of time, you may elect to forgive the debt. Your giving up the expectation of repayment is sufficient for the elimination of the expectation. The person is presumably not expected to repay a debt that has been forgiven. But in general moral expectation is not eliminated simply by people giving up expectations they hold.

Sometimes we might actually be disappointed when a moral expectation attaching to us is eliminated. We might believe that the elimination of an expectation may cause us to develop less than desirable habits or dispositions. If I have developed a tendency to accumulate debts, I may actually be disappointed when other people forgive me a debt. Their act of forgiveness may strike me as something that is likely to reinforce my worst tendencies. I may realize that a tough and unforgiving attitude on their part will be better for me in the long run. Thus, while having my debts forgiven is pleasant, the elimination of the expectation to pay my debts may be disappointing, all things considered.

To summarize, the elimination of moral expectation takes place when we avoid a moral expectation because the expectation ceases to exist or because we eliminate the possibility of its coming into existence. Sometimes an expectation is eliminated because a person is excused from satisfying it; the inability to satisfy it constitutes such an excuse. The possibility of an expectation can be eliminated because someone alters his or her own circumstances in an effort to avoid dealing with it. Sometimes people bring about the elimination of an expectation by altering their environment. Generally the elimination of an expectation is pleasing to the moral agent to whom it would otherwise attach, but in some cases it may be displeasing or disappointing to the agent.

The partial avoidance of a moral expectation consists in avoiding some but not all of what is necessary to bring it about. Suppose that someone's child has a birthday party, and he or she is expected to drive all of the guests home at the conclusion of the party. However, a parent of one guest unexpectedly shows up just prior to the conclusion of the party and offers to drive half of the children home. If this parent follows through on the offer, then the host parent partially avoids the expectation to drive all of the children home. The host parent is now expected to drive only half the children home.

When a moral agent partially avoids an expectation, the agent still has a choice whether to fulfil the part of the expectation that remains. Whether the agent fulfils it or fails to fulfil it, the agent can still be said to have partially avoided the expectation. The possibility also exists that the agent bears less blame through the failure to fulfil it than if the expectation were not partially avoided. If the host parent neglects to drive any of the guests home, a case could be made that the parent's failure is less blameworthy than if the other parent had not driven half of the guests home. If so, the failure to fulfil the partially avoided expectation is less blameworthy than the failure to avoid the original expectation.

Sometimes a moral expectation is partially avoided because of time constraints. Suppose the number of guests at the birthday party is sufficiently large that driving all of them home would take many hours. Several of the guests' parents realize that their children will arrive home very late at night if they do not take the initiative of picking up their children. If some of these parents drive their own children home, then the expectation of the host parent is partially avoided.

The partial avoidance of an expectation may arise out of someone's inability to fulfil it completely. Suppose that each member of a concert band is expected to play his or her assigned music at a public performance. One trumpet player develops a tired embouchure during a piece containing many high notes and cannot play all of the notes. The trumpet player plays as many notes as she can, and makes a pretence out of playing the rest. In this way she partially avoids the expectation to play all of the notes.

The partial avoidance of an expectation due to an inability to fulfil it completely need not be a matter of avoiding the performance of a discrete number of actions or tasks. Sometimes an expectation can be partially avoided because one cannot fulfil it with the quality it requires or deserves. Suppose a student hoping to attend graduate school needs a letter of recommendation from a professor on one day's notice because another professor reneges on his promise to write one. The professor the student approaches informs the student that she is willing to provide the letter of recommendation, but she warns the student that on such short notice the letter will not be prepared with the level of quality and care that such letters normally deserve. If the student agrees to the arrangement on these terms, then the expectation to write a quality letter of recommendation is partially avoided by the professor.

In many situations the level of quality required to fulfil or satisfy a moral expectation is less than clear. A person might argue that if a professor is expected to write a letter of recommendation, then that is exactly what the professor is expected to do and any letter of recommendation fulfils the expectation. Thus, a professor can satisfy the expectation with a minimum of effort, and this is true even if the professor has ample time and opportunity to produce a quality letter of recommendation.

Frequently a moral expectation can be satisfied in a variety of ways, and frequently we can distinguish between the bare satisfaction of an expectation and a more robust satisfaction of the expectation. Some people may have a tendency to dispose of their moral expectations with a minimum expenditure of time and energy, while other people may be more inclined to go beyond the minimal of what is required to satisfy the expectation. Those who make requests of others are wise to clarify what is to count as a satisfactory fulfillment of the expectation. If a student does not wish to settle for a letter of recommendation prepared with a minimum of time and effort, the student would be well advised to indicate as diplomatically as possible that what is desired is a letter of recommendation that goes beyond the bare minimum of what satisfies the expectation to write a letter.

Much has been written about going beyond the call of duty, and perhaps we can speak here about going beyond the call of expectation. Since moral duty is a species of moral expectation, the concept of going beyond the mere requirements of the situation can be broadened to include a great deal more than what is discussed in the literature. It is not just duty that can be satisfied by going beyond the minimal requirements. Someone can go beyond the call of expectation by doing more than what is minimally required to satisfy or fulfil it.

Just as nothing is wrong or blameworthy as such in failing to go beyond the call of duty, nothing is blameworthy as such in failing to go beyond the call of expectation. Instead, going beyond the call of expectation is frequently praiseworthy. To invest more time and effort than what we know to be strictly necessary in bringing about the successful fulfillment of an expectation can be praiseworthy.

Moral philosophers have frequently noted that going beyond the call of duty qualifies as supererogation. An act of supererogation is standardly characterized as an act whose performance is morally praiseworthy and does not fulfil duty and whose non-performance is not morally blameworthy. Acts of heroism and self-sacrifice are often held up as examples of supererogation because they are praiseworthy to perform, they are not (normally) someone's duty or obligation, and nothing is morally blameworthy in omitting to perform them. Here I propose that going beyond the call of expectation can also qualify as behavior which is supererogatory. Just as actions in which someone goes beyond the call of duty can qualify as supererogatory, the same is true of actions in which someone goes beyond the call of (non-obligatory) expectation.

Some philosophers and theologians do not acknowledge the possibility of supererogation or going beyond the call of duty. For a variety of reasons some have taken the position that every act that is morally praiseworthy to perform is at the same time a moral duty. No matter how much self-sacrifice is involved in the praiseworthy performance of an act, we violate duty if we forbear to perform the act. This rejection of the possibility of supererogation involves adherence to a very strict and demanding conception of morality. Applied to moral expectation, this conception of morality instructs us to do our best when fulfilling a moral expectation. We are required to invest whatever time or energy is necessary to do the best job we are capable of doing.

In fact, the anti-supererogationist position, as it is commonly called, is likely to dismiss the entire idea of moral expectation, or at least expectation extending beyond the scope of moral duty. An approach to morality strict enough to regard all praiseworthy behavior as obligatory does not seem likely to countenance the possibility of an act whose omission is blameworthy but not in violation of moral duty. If a person holds that nothing can be praiseworthy beyond moral duty, the person is unlikely to affirm that something can be blameworthy beyond the moral duty to refrain. Thus, the person is unlikely to affirm the possibility of acts which people are morally expected but not required to perform.

For the purposes of this discussion I assume that acts that go beyond the call of duty are possible. I assume that not everything that is morally commendable or praiseworthy is at the same time morally obligatory. Elsewhere I have argued in favor of the plausibility of this assumption, and I have urged that some of the worries philosophers and theologians have had about supererogation can be addressed in ways that do not force someone to embrace an anti-supererogationist position (Mellema, 1991, pp. 61ff). The closely related issue of acknowledging the possibility of acts that are morally blameworthy but not morally obligatory to omit will be addressed in detail in Chapter Nine.

Although going beyond the call of moral expectation is never blameworthy as such, a word of caution is in order. Suppose we adopt the habit of fulfilling or discharging our expectations with a minimum of time and effort. Whenever we are faced with a moral expectation, we calculate the most efficient and effortless means of fulfilling it. With respect to each individual instance of fulfilling our moral expectations, no basis for ascribing moral blame is possible. As observed earlier, nothing is blameworthy as such in failing to go beyond the call of expectation. But a larger issue is at stake, namely, the moral evaluation of our resolve to aim for the minimum expenditure of time and effort. Although each individual instance escapes being morally blameworthy, we cannot conclude that the overall resolve escapes the charge of blame.

Frequently the actions we perform to fulfill moral expectation benefit others. People are frequently expected to do that which promotes good for the sake of others. We can perform actions that satisfy these expectations in a spirit of good will, and we can do so in a begrudging spirit. Although the expectation to perform these acts may not include performing them cheerfully, something is wrong with a person who invariably approaches them with a spirit of grudging resignation combined with a desire to dispose of them with as little time and energy as possible. This type of attitude regarding moral expectation is missing something important in its approach to living the moral life. Perhaps this attitude can be characterized from an aretaic point of view as lacking in virtue or even infected with moral vice. Alternatively, a person who approaches moral expectation in this manner is possibly failing to fulfil a higher order moral expectation that we should not always carry out our expectations with a bare minimum of time and effort.

To summarize, an agent can be said to partially avoid an expectation when the agent avoids some but not all of what is necessary to fulfil it. The partial avoidance of an expectation can take the form of being expected to perform fewer actions or tasks than originally necessary or a lowering of expectations concerning the quality of our performance of actions or tasks. Frequently a distinction can be made between the bare satisfaction of an expectation and going beyond the minimal of what is necessary to satisfy the expectation. The latter can qualify as supererogatory. While nothing is blameworthy as such in pursuing the minimal course of action in satisfying our expectations, something may be wrong with making a habit or practice of doing so.

Seven

GROUP EXPECTATION

The discussion up to this point has been confined to what an individual moral agent can be expected to do. My contention in this chapter is that groups of two or more agents can be morally expected to perform actions or bring about states of affairs. In addition, groups can be morally expected to omit or refrain from performing a particular action or from bringing about a state of affairs. Later in the chapter I examine situations in which groups fail to carry out these expectations, particularly situations in which members of a group bear varying degrees of moral blame for the failure to carry out these expectations.

A simple, straightforward case of group expectation consists in the expectation that two people perform an action that neither person can perform alone. Two teenagers can be expected to carry their mother's newly purchased washing machine from the driveway into their basement. And two people who have agreed to perform an instrumental duet during a worship service can be expected to perform the duet at the appropriate time.

Some philosophers have been reluctant to acknowledge the possibility of joint or group actions, but examples such as these can be described without reference to joint actions by referring instead to the outcomes of their individual actions. The teenagers are expected to bring about the outcome of the washing machine's being in the basement through their individual actions, and those agreeing to perform a duet are expected to bring about its performance through their individual actions. Either way, these are straightforward cases of group expectation.

Another straightforward type of group expectation involves two or more individuals simultaneously performing actions aimed toward identical outcomes. If a classroom teacher instructs the students to spend the next ten minutes working on a particular problem in their exercise booklets, the students can be expected to do exactly that. Each student is expected to spend the time working on this problem. Some students may fail to solve the problem in the ten minute interval, but they nevertheless perform actions aimed at achieving the solution of the problem.

Sometimes group expectation involves several people simultaneously performing actions to bring about a single outcome, a situation that can sometimes be described in terms of reciprocal expectations (Kutz, 2001, p. 456). Suppose a classroom teacher instructs the students to spend the next hour working on a mural depicting a certain theme. Each student is expected to paint scenes somewhere on the mural that depict or contribute to depicting an aspect of this theme. The finished mural then consists of many scenes painted by many students.

All of the examples so far presented have involved two or more individuals performing actions during the same interval of time. The situation becomes slightly more complicated when the group expectation is fulfilled by people acting at different times. Imagine that the residents of one cabin in a summer camp are assigned the task of weeding a garden. Their counselor informs them of the task and assigns each resident of the cabin to spend a half hour of weeding to be completed by supper time. Each camper proceeds to weed for a half hour, but the campers do not all weed during the same half hour. Some elect to begin at once, others postpone their weeding for a short while, and some elect to postpone their weeding until the last possible time interval. But by suppertime all of the campers have completed a half hour of work, and the group expectation is fulfilled.

This example involves many people performing the same task in the same location during varying intervals of time. But clearly the example could be altered so that it no longer contains uniformity of tasks or uniformity of location. The campers could choose to work in the garden for a half hour in some capacity other than weeding and thereby satisfy the group expectation. Or the campers could choose to spend a half hour weeding in one of several locations and thereby satisfy the group expectation. Moreover, the uniformity of tasks and uniformity of location features could both be removed if the campers were allowed to choose both the task and the location. As long as all of them work for a half hour on some approved task at one approved location, the group expectation is fulfilled.

Sometimes the fulfillment of a group expectation requires that its members perform a series of acts. Suppose that the members of a group have agreed to provide around-the-clock observation of a person who is seriously ill and cannot be left alone. A schedule is drawn up, and each member is assigned an interval of time each day to be present. The expectation that the patient receives continuous observation is carried out if each member is present at his or her scheduled time and remains present through the designated interval of time. In this way, the fulfillment of the group expectation requires its members to perform a series of acts.

Sometimes which members of a group have to act to fulfil or satisfy a group expectation is less than clear. On some occasions the group expectation is fulfilled by the performance of an action by one of its members. Suppose that a committee is meeting behind locked doors to discuss some confidential business matters. If one member of the committee arrives late and begins to knock on the door, the committee members can be expected to open the door and allow this member to enter the room. The fulfillment of this expectation does not require action by all of the members; it is fulfilled by one member's opening the door. One member volunteers to perform the required action, and the group expectation is fulfilled.

If no one volunteers to open the door for the late committee member, the committee may wish to adopt a decision procedure to determine who opens the door. Perhaps the committee decides that the member with the least seniority must get up and open the door. If no one volunteers, the committee may simply decide that no one will open the door. In this case the group expectation is not fulfilled, and the late member is forced to miss the meeting in its entirety for want of someone willing to open the door. This outcome's taking place is unlikely, for opening the door is an action that involves relatively little effort.

Nevertheless, a group expectation might require one member to perform an act of considerable risk. If so, no one might volunteer to perform the act. Imagine that a child who is about to drown is calling for help, and a shark is known to be nearby. On the shore are twenty people; none is a lifeguard, but they are equally capable of performing the rescue. We can expect of this group that one of its members perform the rescue. If some of the twenty do not know of the presence of the shark, one of them might undertake the rescue. But if all twenty know of the presence of the shark, no one might volunteer to perform the rescue and the expectation that the child be rescued is not carried out.

Another type of situation in which no one might volunteer to perform the act which satisfies a group expectation is a situation where the act requires a great deal of self-sacrifice. For example, in the lobby of a public building a homeless man suddenly points a loaded revolver at the head of a woman walking near him and begins shouting to the bystanders. He announces that he will fire the weapon at this woman unless someone steps forward and agrees to provide him with food and shelter until he can get his life back together. Several of the bystanders have enough room in their homes or enough money to rent him a room to meet his demand, and these bystanders can be expected to take action so as not to allow the woman to be shot by the homeless man.

But conceivably none of them steps forward and volunteers. Aside from the factor of risk (he may be dangerous), none of the bystanders may be eager to make the personal or financial sacrifices required to support the man until he can get his life back together. This type of support could involve a long-term commitment. Under the circumstances each bystander might wait for someone else to step forward, and in the end no one may volunteer.

Group expectation might require action by more than one person but less than all of the persons comprising the group. Suppose that the employees of a small company have indicated a willingness to help out at an event to raise money for a local charity, and they subsequently learn that three people from their office are scheduled to help out on a particular day. In this situation the employees can be expected to provide three of their number for this day. Coming up with three volunteers might be relatively easy, for doing so may involve a day away from the office performing tasks which are pleasant and entertaining.

Nevertheless, this need not be the case. As before, volunteering can involve risk or self-sacrifice. The employees of this small company might learn that the volunteers from the charity event will be forced to use one of their precious vacation days or that the day they are needed to help out is a weekend day. They will be much less enthusiastic about volunteering if they must sacrifice a vacation day or a day from their weekend. In the end, producing three volunteers for this event could be difficult. If fewer than three are sent to help out, the group expectation is not fulfilled.

In each of the cases so far examined a definite number of people are required to perform actions on behalf of the group. But group expectation does not always require a precise minimum number of people performing these actions. Perhaps the organizers of the charity event fail to specify a precise number of volunteers from the company. The instructions received by the company may simply state that a few or several employees should appear on a certain day. The company is then left with some discretion as to the number of employees it provides on that day. The precise number is underdetermined by the instructions. Presumably the company should provide more than one employee, but how many more should be provided is less than clear.

Another type of case in which the number of people required to fulfil the group expectation is unclear or indeterminate is where the specification is made in terms of actions to be performed. The organizers of the charity event might specify that two booths need to be covered by the employees of the company for an entire day and leave the company to decide how many people are required to perform the tasks involved in covering two booths for an entire day. As long as people from the company are present at both booths for the day, the group expectation has been satisfied.

Sometimes group expectation requires one or more members of the group to refrain from action. The members of a church might host a hunger awareness dinner in which a certain number of participants are expected to refrain from eating to dramatize the fact that a considerable percentage of the world's population does not have enough food to eat. Imagine that the number of people who volunteer to sit through the dinner without food must be a ratio of those present to match this percentage. If all of the people coming to the event are aware of the procedure, a certain number of the group can be expected to sit through the meal with an empty plate. Those who volunteer, provided they constitute a sufficient number, satisfy the group expectation by their refraining from partaking of the food.

To summarize, group expectation can take different forms. Sometimes the fulfillment of the expectation requires that all members of the group take action. The action can be in the form of a group action, individual actions aimed toward identical outcomes, or individual actions aimed toward a diversity of outcomes, whether simultaneous or at differing times. Sometimes the group expectation can be fulfilled by one group's members taking action, and sometimes the group expectation can be fulfilled by several but fewer than all of the members, taking action. The number required may or may not be a precise number. In cases of this type one or more members may volunteer to perform the appropriate actions on behalf of the group. Whether people are motivated to volunteer may depend upon the actions to be performed. People will be less inclined to volunteer to perform actions whose performance involves considerable risk or self-sacrifice. Finally, group expectation sometimes requires that a certain number of its members refrain from action.

The discussion of group expectation has focused upon the satisfaction or fulfillment of expectations that attach to the group. I turn now to a consideration of a group's failure to fulfil an expectation that attaches to it. The interpersonal dynamics involved in the failure of group expectation raise many moral issues not raised in the case of an individual's failure to fulfil a moral expectation. In what follows I call attention to some of these issues and in doing so I hope to shed further light upon the nature of moral expectation.

In earlier chapters the failure of an agent to fulfil a moral expectation was characterized as morally blameworthy. And not only is the failure morally blameworthy, but the agent is morally blameworthy for this failure. Such a failure is always morally blameworthy to at least a small degree. The degree to which the failure is blameworthy will depend upon a variety of factors, such as whether the failure is deliberate, the agent's motives, state of mind, or character defects, the degree of difficulty in fulfilling the expectation, and so forth. When the moral expectation is at the same time a moral obligation, the failure is serious enough to be described as morally impermissible, and the degree of blame is affected significantly.

Some may be inclined to assign blame directly to a group that fails to carry out a moral expectation. For the purposes of this discussion, I will speak only of the blame that attaches to the individual members of the group. Of particular interest are factors that appear to render some of these individuals as more blameworthy than others when a group fails to carry out a moral expectation. What is of concern in this discussion is the blame each individual bears for the failure of the group, not necessarily the blame each member bears for his or her own failure to act toward the success of the group project.

One factor capable of causing differences in the degree to which various members are morally blameworthy for the group failure is intent. Those who intentionally refrain from doing their part in fulfilling the group expectation tend to be more blameworthy, other things being equal, than those who do so unintentionally. Unintentional refraining may be the result of forgetfulness, fear, ignorance, or threats. Recall the example in which the campers in a certain cabin are assigned the task of spending a half hour weeding in the garden. If only a handful of these campers do their part, the group has failed to carry out what is expected of it. However, among the individuals who bear moral blame, namely, those who fail to do their part, can be differences in the degree of blame. Those who deliberately thumb their nose at the assignment are presumably more to blame for the overall outcome than those who forget to carry out their assigned task.

Another factor that accounts for differences in the degree of blame which members bear for a group failure is the difference of contribution by different members toward the outcome (where the contribution under discussion is not limited to causal contribution). Several individual failures contributing to differing degrees to an overall group failure might initially seem puzzling. But a moment's reflection will show that in many situations variability of contribution is possible. While those campers who do no weeding seem to contribute equally to the group failure, the same is not true of those who work less than the assigned half hour. Suppose that some of the campers do no weeding, some of the campers weed their allotted thirty minutes, and several campers begin pulling weeds in the garden and decide to leave after fifteen minutes. In this scenario the members who do no work are more to blame for the group failure than those who at least spend fifteen minutes pulling weeds.

In some situations variability of contribution takes place where the members of a group are expected to refrain from action, and at least some of the members do not refrain. The employees of a store that sells candy in bulk quantities are told that under no circumstances may they help themselves to the candy. Some of the employees faithfully refrain from taking candy, and some of the employees help themselves to candy. Most of the employees who help themselves to candy do so only minimally on an occasional basis. But one employee helps himself to considerable quantities of candy and manages to do so undetected. The owner of the store realizes that some of the merchandise is unaccounted for and comes to the realization that the employees have failed to fulfil the expectation to refrain from helping themselves to the candy.

The employees who bear blame for the failure of the group expectation are those who have taken candy. However, among these employees is a considerable disparity in the degree to which they contribute to the outcome. One employee is responsible for the vast majority of the missing candy, and hence he bears more blame for the group failure than the others who have taken candy.

When the members of a group perform acts at differing times, variation in the degree to which they are blameworthy for a group failure is also possible. Suppose that the workers in the office of a tele-marketing firm are allowed to take ten minute breaks during the morning. They are allowed to take their breaks whenever they wish to do so, but they are aware of a firm expectation that no one's break exceeds ten minutes and no more than three workers are on break simultaneously. The workers can easily see one another, and seeing how many are on break at any given time is a simple matter.

One day three workers are on break, and a fourth worker joins them. They are quite surprised and alarmed, they remind this worker of the office policy and they tell him that he must go back to work. Suppose he refuses on the grounds that some of them have been on break for longer than ten minutes, and suppose that this is the case. One has been there twenty minutes, one has been there fifteen minutes, and one has been there five minutes. Who, then, is blame-worthy for the failure of the group to abide by the expectation?

Surely the one who has been on break for five minutes bears no blame for the group failure. The other workers have not acted in conformity with the office policy, and their joint actions are sufficient for the failure of the group expecta-tion. But if each bears blame for this group failure, the worker on break for twenty minutes is arguably more blameworthy than the worker on break for fifteen min-utes. Intuitions may vary concerning the fourth worker, but a case can be made that he might be judged more blameworthy than the other two on the grounds that his actions cause a shortage of the workers on duty. Nevertheless, even so, the other two clearly bear differing degrees of blame from one another.

Special problems arise in situations where the members of a group perform a series of actions in which a threshold is crossed. The members of the group are expected, to refrain from performing too many acts of a certain type, because an unwanted outcome will be likely to occur once a threshold has been crossed. As David Lyons has pointed out, the threshold need not be a precise number (Lyons, 1965, p. 72). But too many acts of a certain type produce an unwanted outcome, and the members of a group are expected to avoid producing or causing the out-come by paying attention to the number of acts performed by its members.

An example of this phenomenon can be found in a situation where a foot-bridge is present in a heavily visited nature preserve. A sign at both ends of the bridge warns that no more than two persons should set foot on the bridge simul-taneously. The clear implication is that the bridge is likely to collapse if three or more persons occupy it at the same time. Suppose that a group of college stu-dents is visiting the nature preserve, and the students decide to test the limits of the bridge. One by one the students walk onto the bridge and remain standing on it. The bridge does not collapse when the third student sets foot on it, nor does it collapse when the fourth student sets foot on it. But with the advent of the fifth student the bridge slowly collapses until it comes to rest in a small stream. Thereafter, several more students walk out on the now collapsed bridge.

The college students, like all visitors to the nature preserve, are expected to obey the instructions and not take actions that result in three persons occupy-ing the bridge at the same time. Hence these college students are blameworthy for the outcome. But are they all blameworthy? The first two students to walk onto the bridge may argue for their innocence on the grounds that their actions in no way violate the instructions posted on the bridge. The students walking onto the already collapsed bridge argue for their innocence on the grounds that no point can be found in obeying the instructions once the bridge collapses. The third and fourth students to walk onto the bridge concede that their actions are not in accord with the instructions, but they consider their actions less blame-worthy than those of the fifth student who causes the actual collapse of the bridge to take place. On this line of reasoning, the person who crosses the thresh-old through the performance of his or her act bears more blame, other things being equal, than the persons acting prior in the sequence or the persons acting later in the sequence.

Three main questions that surface in scenarios of this type are the following. First, does each member performing an act make an equal contribution to the outcome and hence bear equal blame for the outcome? Second, if the first question is answered in the negative, does the person whose action triggers the threshold bear more blame, other things being equal, than the persons acting prior in the sequence? Third, if the first question is answered in the negative, does the person whose action triggers the threshold bear more blame, other things being equal, than the persons acting later in the sequence?

In his article, "On Causal Consequences" R. G. Frey discusses some of these issues and coins the term "equalizer" to describe someone who believes that each member acting in a sequence where the acts are nearly identical makes an equal contribution to the outcome. Thus, an equalizer will give an affirmative answer to question one. After an extended discussion of these issues Frey appears to reject the equalizer view. He finds difficulty maintaining that the acts that occur after the threshold has been crossed contribute to the outcome to a degree equal to that of the preceding acts in the sequence (Frey, 1974, p. 375). And to see how they contribute causally to the outcome at all is difficult. The discussion of Frey does not raise the issue of blame, and hence he does not directly consider anything along the lines of question three. But an affirmation of question three appears to be in the spirit of Frey's remarks.

Another philosopher who has considered these issues is Michael J. Zimmerman. He constructs an example in which each of a dozen people delivers one stab to the body of a victim. The action of each person is causally necessary for the death of the victim, but the victim dies only after the final and twelfth stab. Thus, the threshold occurs on the occasion of the stab delivered by the twelfth assailant. Zimmerman believes that some will be inclined to regard the twelfth stab as unique among the actions in the sequence, for it is the final assailant who delivers the *coup de grace*. But he is not persuaded that the final act is significantly different than the others (Zimmerman, 1985, p. 118).

For Zimmerman the point of importance is that each act in the sequence is causally necessary for the outcome. Like Frey, he does not raise the issue of blame in the context of this discussion, and he does not consider any questions such as those under consideration here. But a negative answer to question two appears to be in the spirit of his views, at least with regard to examples of the type he considers. We have no reason to regard the twelfth assailant as more blameworthy than the other assailants.

The example of the footbridge differs from the example of the stabbed victim in several important respects, one of which is that being the first to walk on the bridge is an act of innocence in a way that being the first to stab the victim is not. Hence we can accept Zimmerman's verdict concerning his example and maintain that the first two students setting foot on the bridge are less to blame than the third, fourth, or fifth students. And we can maintain this view even if we acknowledge that the first two students are somewhat to blame for participating in the group plan to test the limits of the bridge and for remaining on the bridge when too many others join them.

Zimmerman goes on to consider a revised version of the stabbing example by introducing a thirteenth assailant. This assailant stabs the victim just as the previous twelve stab the victim, but the situation is quite different in that the victim is already dead prior to the advent of the thirteenth assailant. Thus, the threshold has already been crossed when this assailant acts. Zimmerman believes that the actions of the thirteenth assailant are significantly different from the actions of the others; unlike the actions of the previous twelve, these actions are not causally necessary for the death of the victim (*Ibid.*, p. 120). Zimmerman makes clear, however, that he is assuming that the thirteenth assailant is not involved in a plot or conspiracy with the other twelve.

On the basis of these remarks, Zimmerman can plausibly be judged to reject the equalizer view. Although he agrees with the equalizer that the first eleven assailants contribute to the outcome no less than the twelfth assailant, the one who triggers the threshold, he rejects the view that those who act subsequent to the crossing of the threshold contribute to the outcome equally to those acting earlier in the sequence. On this point he is in agreement with Frey; accordingly, an affirmative answer to question three is in the spirit of what he says about the thirteenth assailant. Regarding the example of the footbridge, we could accept the views of Frey and Zimmerman and thus regard the students stepping on the already collapsed bridge as less blameworthy than those acting earlier in the sequence. And we could accept this verdict even if we find that these students do not entirely escape blame due to their participation in the plan to test the limits of the bridge.

In situations where the order in which the members of a group performing a series of actions is simply a matter of luck, a case can be made that moral luck is present. If Zimmerman and Frey are correct about those acting after the threshold is crossed, and if offering an affirmative answer to question three is correct, then a person can regard it as a matter of luck that he or she performs an act in the series after the threshold is crossed and thereby incurs less moral blame. By being lucky enough to perform an act at this point in the sequence, the person is lucky to bear less blame than otherwise. Those who reject the possibility of moral luck will be less than convinced that moral luck is present in situations of this type. But for those who do not reject its possibility, the relevance of moral luck at this point of the discussion is worth noting.

A related question taken up by Zimmerman concerning the variability of blame among the members of a group is whether the size of the group has a bearing on the degree of each member's blame. In Zimmerman's example the actions of twelve people are causally necessary for the occurrence of the outcome. Is the degree of blame borne by each person affected by the number involved? Suppose that each of one hundred assailants stabs the victim, and the threshold is crossed at the point of the stabbing by the one hundredth assailant. As before, the group expectation to refrain from killing the victim is not fulfilled, but the size of the group is now dramatically increased. Is the degree of blame borne by each assailant for the victim's death diluted or diminished as the result of expanding the size of the group?

I believe that people are commonly inclined to assume that the larger the group which contributes causally to the outcome, the smaller the degree of blame which each member bears for the outcome. The idea is that only so much moral blame is present to be apportioned among the members, and we can lessen our own share of the blame by making efforts to enlarge the number of people performing actions of the requisite sort. If one hundred assailants deliver stabs to the victim, then, on this way of thinking, the stab of each is less consequential and morally significant than if twelve are involved. This way of thinking has some intuitive appeal, it appears to be operative to some extent among people who are employed in formal organizations, including governmental organizations, and it has been defended in the philosophical literature.

The idea that the degree of blame varies according to the number of people involved together with the idea that only so much blame is present to go around has not been universally accepted. Zimmerman states his opposition to these ideas in the context of moral responsibility. He rejects the idea that just so much responsibility is present to go around, and he rejects the idea that the more people involved, the smaller the share apportioned to each. He opposes the idea that moral responsibility can be thought of as a pie, according to which someone's slice of the pie becomes smaller when the number of people involved becomes greater (*Ibid.*, p. 115). Robert Nozick makes a similar point by denying that moral responsibility can be compared to a bucket. The contents of a bucket are limited, and only so much can be apportioned to those desiring water from the bucket. But he believes we would be mistaken to think in the same way about responsibility; we would be mistaken to think that less responsibility remains when some of it is apportioned to various people (Nozick, 1974, p. 130). Analogies of this type also appear to be rejected in the work of Derek Parfit (Parfit, 1984, p. 80).

These philosophers, then, hold that someone's moral responsibility for a state of affairs is not affected by the sheer size of the group consisting of those bearing responsibility for the same state of affairs. Applied to moral expectation, this opposition to the pie or bucket analogy would amount to the view that not just so much blame is present to be apportioned to those whose actions account for the failure of the group expectation. Accordingly, the size of the group does not have a direct impact upon the degree to which each of its members bears moral blame for the outcome. Specifically, the degree of blame borne by each member is not diluted or diminished as the group increases in size.

The degree to which someone bears moral blame for the failure of a group expectation can nevertheless be influenced by the actions of other members.

Suppose that several friends are conspiring to play a prank that involves defacing a public work of art. One member of the group is reluctant to participate in this plan and announces his intention to decline participating in defacing the work of art. The others are upset with this member and threaten him with the termination of their friendship if he refuses to participate. Consequently, he participates in the prank with great reluctance. In this example we might plausibly conclude that the degree to which he bears blame for the outcome is less than if he were an enthusiastic participant. The threats by the others cause the degree of his blame to be less than it would otherwise be. At the same time, the threats cause him to bear a higher degree of blame than if he did not participate at all. In any case, the degree of blame he bears is affected by the actions of the other members.

A variant of this example shows that the number of participants can have an impact upon the degree of one's blame for the outcome. In this example all the friends are enthusiastic about the plan to deface the work of art. However, when they are about to begin several bystanders decide to join them. Suddenly the group of those defacing the work of art expands in size, and some of the group of friends are less than pleased by this development. They view this as their project, resent the intrusion of additional uninvited participants, and one of the original group in fact walks away and does not deface the work of art. We might claim that this is an example in which the degree of one member's blame is diminished as the result of expanding the number of participants, for the person who walks away and does not deface the work of art surely bears less blame than if he had joined the others.

Nevertheless, opponents of the view that the degree of someone's blame diminishes as the size of the group increases might not be persuaded by this claim. They can argue that in this example the expansion of the group does not as such reduce the degree of blame borne by the member who walks away and does not participate. After all, no apparent diluting of blame borne by the members of the original group who participate in defacing the work of art occurs. The expansion of the group indirectly causes the member who walks away to bear less blame for the outcome, but what is crucial in this example is his own decision to walk away because he resents the intrusion of the bystanders. Thus, the expansion of the group does not itself cause dilution of his blame for the failure of the group expectation.

Many people have a tendency to assume that in any given situation only so much blame is present to go around, and their share of the blame diminishes as more people bear blame for the same group failure. Others, like Zimmerman, Nozick, and Parfit, argue that this is not the case. While we have difficulty finding an example which shows decisively that the reduction of someone's degree of blame is the direct result of a group's increasing in size, we likewise have difficulty offering an argument which constitutes an outright refutation of the dilutionist thesis or the inappropriateness of the pie or bucket analogies.

To summarize, when a group fails to carry out a moral expectation some or all of the members of the group bear moral blame for this failure. Those bearing moral blame sometimes bear an equal degree of blame for the group failure, but in many cases they bear varying degrees of blame for the group failure. One factor capable of causing varying degrees of blame is intent. A person who intentionally refrains from doing his or her part in fulfilling the group expectation is likely to bear more blame, other things being equal, than a person who does so unintentionally. Other factors which gives rise to varying degrees of blame for the group failure include the difference of contribution by various members of the group toward the outcome and differences in the times at which members perform acts which contribute toward the outcome.

Of special interest are situations where the members of a group perform acts in a series in which the outcome is produced at the point where a threshold is crossed. We can reasonably regard the degree of blame of those performing acts after the threshold has been crossed as less than that of the person whose act triggers the threshold, for their acts do not contribute causally to the outcome. Whether acts performed prior to the crossing of the threshold contribute to the outcome equal to the contribution of acts that trigger the threshold is less clear. Finally, many believe that the degree of blame someone bears for a group failure is diminished or diluted as the number of people similarly bearing blame for the group failure increases. This belief is typically based on the assumption that for any group failure only so much blame can go around. Although offering an outright refutation of these beliefs is difficult, they are certainly open to question and have been challenged in the literature.

Eight

THE SYMBOLIC DIMENSION

In this chapter I develop the idea that expectation has a symbolic dimension. The communication of a moral expectation, the acknowledgement of a moral expectation, the fulfillment of a moral expectation, the promise to fulfil a moral expectation, and the refusal to fulfil a moral expectation are all actions whose meaning or significance can be readily apparent to observers. However, in addition to the straightforward meaning or significance of these actions, much can be symbolized by their performance.

The symbolic dimension of moral expectation can best be approached by appealing to Robert Nozick's notion of symbolic utility. The first half of this chapter is devoted to presenting and explicating this notion. In the second half of this chapter I make use of symbolic utility to discover and explore the symbolic aspects of moral expectation (predictive expectation also has a symbolic dimension, but I will focus on moral expectation). In doing so I hope to deepen and enrich our knowledge of moral expectation and the role it plays in the lives of moral agents.

Nozick introduces the notion of symbolic utility in his book, *The Nature of Rationality*. Although much has been written about symbolism and symbolic meaning, Nozick breaks important new ground in showing how the moral status of an act can be affected by what is symbolized by the performance of an act. His work is significant, in large part, because it brings together two areas of philosophy, ethics and the philosophy of language, in a manner that has strong potential for shedding light upon both areas.

Since the concept of utility is the focal point of Nozick's discussion, what he says about symbolic utility has a decidedly consequentialist emphasis. I hope to show that the concept of symbolic utility can be useful in understanding other areas of morality, such as virtue ethics and, of course, moral expectation. Because the term "symbolic utility" carries with it strong consequentialist connotations and its sphere of application is wider than considerations of utility, I will employ the more neutral terminology of the "symbolic value" of an act throughout the remainder of the discussion.

The basic idea of the symbolic value of an act is relatively straightforward: the performance of one act can symbolize the actual or potential performances of other acts or states of affairs in a manner that has moral significance. Roughly speaking, moral value, whether positive or negative, is produced as the result of the symbolization. As Nozick puts it, value "flows back" along symbolic (as opposed to causal) lines from the future acts in the series to the original act (Nozick, 1993, p. 27). The notion of symbolic value as articulated here is considerably narrower than the relation of ordinary symbolization. Communicating to a deaf person through the use of sign language involves performing acts that symbolize various states of affairs. But these states of affairs would ordinarily not qualify as the symbolic value of the acts which are performed, for no moral dimension as such is built into the practice of communicating through sign language. Thus, Nozick's key insight is that the linguistic concept of symbolization has a rich moral component, one which has been explored neither by philosophers of language nor by moral philosophers.

A simple example of symbolic value can be seen in the practice of promising. Making a promise symbolizes the future act of carrying out the promise, and this is so regardless of whether the promise is actually carried out. Another simple example is raising a hand when volunteers are being solicited to perform a task. This action symbolizes the future act of performing the task. In each of these examples is an implicit moral dimension: breaking a promise is morally blameworthy, volunteering is morally praiseworthy, but volunteering and not following through is morally blameworthy.

Promising and volunteering are actions whose symbolic value depends upon the presence of conventions. Because conventions are in place, people who make promises or volunteer for certain activities are expected to follow through. Sometimes the presence of these conventions confers upon otherwise mundane acts a high degree of significance, as with the symbolic value created by placing a ring upon another's finger when it occurs in the context of a wedding ceremony or the symbolic value created by acts performed in the context of religious ceremonies.

However, recognizing that symbolic value can likewise take place in the absence of conventions is important. In general, we can distinguish two kinds of symbolism: symbolism that depends upon the presence of conventions and symbolism which does not. When someone's small child performs an act of generosity, the symbolic value can consist in its symbolizing a pattern of acts of generosity extending into the future. The act of generosity simply represents actions of a similar sort, and the child's parents can derive great satisfaction as the result of this representation. But this representation takes place not because it falls within the context of certain conventions. It takes place because one act can stand for or symbolize other acts that are relevantly similar.

The symbolic value of an act is not normally the same as a disposition to act. If I volunteer to perform a task, my act of volunteering may signify a willingness to perform the task (and it may also signify a willingness to volunteer for tasks). However, what is signified by an act is not in general identical to the symbolic value of an act. In special cases the symbolic value may consist at least in part of dispositions to act, as when I promise to be willing to do something. But the disposition signified by an act is not necessarily its symbolic value.

Part of what determines the symbolic value of an act is the agent's intent in performing the act, but it is also determined in part by the perception of the act by others. Suppose that a man who has been convicted of a heinous crime is sentenced by a judge to twenty hours of community service. Because the public perception is that the judge has been far too lenient, the act may serve to symbolize future ludicrously lenient sentences to other convicted criminals. But this symbolic value need not reflect the intent of the judge, for the judge may have no intent to issue lenient sentences in the future.

Discussing the relevance of symbolic value to virtue ethics will be helpful in understanding its relevance to moral expectation. When a person performs a single act of virtue this act can symbolize or stand for other potential acts of the virtue in question. For that matter, it can symbolize acts of other virtues, but here I will concentrate upon virtues or vices one at a time. According to an Aristotelian account of moral virtue, an agent can acquire a moral virtue, in part, by practicing the virtue, that is, by performing a series of acts exemplifying the virtue. And we could say of one particular act in this series that it symbolizes the performance of the others in this series. When a just person performs a just act, this act can symbolize a lifetime of just acts performed by this person.

But not all acts of justice are performed by just persons or even by persons who are on their way to becoming just persons, and here Nozick's ideas begin to be helpful. When a person performs a single just act, this act can symbolize the potential performance of other just acts. And these potential performances need not be actual performances. Whether or not the person ever performs another just act, the performance of this just act symbolizes the performance of other potential just acts by the same person. Part of what is gratifying about a single act of virtue is that it symbolizes something larger than itself, the possibility of additional future acts of the virtue by the same person. The symbolic value of the act encourages us to think in terms of a pattern extending into the future, and we can think in terms of this pattern whether or not it actually occurs.

Similarly, a single act of vice can symbolize a pattern of acts of this particular vice extending into the future. A single act of rudeness can symbolize a pattern of rude actions by the person performing it. Depending upon the circumstances, this can be the cause of concern or even alarm. But the potential acts of rudeness symbolized by the single act of rudeness need not actually be performed.

The picture becomes more complicated when the concept of symbolic value is applied to series of acts performed by more than one agent. The performance of an act of virtue or vice can symbolize additional acts of the same virtue or vice by several agents. To take a simple example, we criticize someone's throwing a gum wrapper on an otherwise immaculate park lawn. If the person is a chronic litterer, our criticism may be rooted in the act's proceeding from a fixed and unchangeable disposition, to use Aristotelian terminology. But if the person is not a habitual litterer, nor thought to be one, we must look in a different direction for the source of our moral displeasure. I suggest that the act of throwing a gum wrapper on the lawn symbolizes a series of similar acts by a variety of people, with the end result that the park becomes filled with litter. The act is viewed as a part of a possible or potential pattern based not on a series of acts by one individual but on a series of acts by many individuals.

The possibility of ascribing virtue or vice to a series of acts by more than one agent is a phenomenon which is recognized in ordinary discourse. When someone claims to have been treated rudely by the clerks in a certain store, we can interpret this claim as ascribing rudeness to a pattern of acts by different clerks. Just as we take note of a pattern of rude acts by one individual over time, we sometimes take note of a pattern of rude acts by various agents. The notion of symbolic value accommodates this intuition. It allows for the possibility of speaking about a virtuous or vicious pattern of behavior involving more than one moral agent, and it allows us to see a connection between a single act of virtue by one moral agent and a pattern of virtuous acts by many moral agents.

An act of virtue or vice not only can symbolize a virtuous or vicious pattern of behavior by several agents, but it can also by extension symbolize a foreseeable outcome produced by this pattern. Thus, the single act of littering not only symbolizes a potential pattern of littering, but it conjures up images of a park with great quantities of litter.

An awareness of this phenomenon can shed light upon the practice known as scapegoating. When something unfortunate or inconvenient happens, we sometimes have a tendency to single out someone as the scapegoat for this state of affairs. Perhaps an act of vice by this person can be identified as tangentially related to the unfortunate event, and a condemnation of this act of vice provides a way for people to vent their rage or frustration when other factors leading to the unfortunate event are not known. The act of vice symbolizes similar acts of vice by other unknown individuals, and it ultimately symbolizes the unfortunate state of affairs that results.

Something is manifestly unfair about the practice of scapegoating, and some might feel that scapegoating itself qualifies as a moral vice. But the point of the present discussion is that the practice of scapegoating is built upon recognizing the symbolic value of an act of vice. We focus upon a single act of vice, and this act symbolizes other actions of vice by the same person or different persons and ultimately the unwanted outcome. Again, Nozick's model enables us to deepen our understanding of a phenomenon from the moral sphere by applying tools developed in the sphere of language.

The opposite practice, singling out someone as the object of praise for a beneficial state of affairs when the person's act of virtue is only tangentially connected to the outcome as a whole, appears to occur less frequently. But this situation can likewise be characterized in terms of symbolic value. People focus upon a single act of virtue and allow it to symbolize other unknown acts of virtue. When many survivors are rescued at the scene of a disaster, one rescuer may emerge as a hero because his or her act of virtue happens to be captured by a press photographer. The heroism of this rescuer comes to symbolize the heroism of many rescuers and the successful rescue itself, and it thereby provides the focal point for the feelings of gratitude that are experienced.

Symbolic value is also helpful in understanding some of the dynamics of groups or collectives. Suppose that a club is committed to an ideology of racism, and one of its members performs an act of racism. This act of racism, then, is symbolic of potential acts of racism by other members. In this sense the single act of racism reflects upon other members, even though they may never have actually performed an act of racism. Even if we do not come to bear moral responsibility for what another member of our group has done, we are linked by membership in the group to the actions of the other.

People sometimes claim to experience collective guilt for an act of vice committed by one or more of the members of a group or collective. On a superficial level experiencing guilt for what another has done may seem irrational. But here too the notion of symbolic value is helpful: if this member's act of vice is genuinely symbolic of what the other members might do, then feeling a certain type of guilt may be perfectly reasonable. If a fellow member of someone's group commits an act of racism, feelings of collective guilt by other members may be reasonable. And part of what makes these feelings reasonable or understandable is the symbolic value of the act. If we think strictly in terms of causal connections, the notion of collective guilt can seem to make little sense (how can an agent bear guilt for something he or she did not in any sense bring about?). But if we recognize the value that flows back along symbolic lines, an entirely different perspective on collective guilt emerges.

In another way symbolic value is operative in the performance of an act of virtue or vice by a member of a collective. Elsewhere I have argued that a collective is morally responsible for a state of affairs only if each member of a collective performs a contributing act, an act by virtue of whose performance he or she comes to have membership in the collective (Mellema, 1997, pp. 112–114). According to this view someone must actually do something or omit to do something to be part of a group that is collectively responsible for an outcome (although the person is not necessarily rendered morally responsible as an individual for this outcome by his or her contributing act). Collective responsibility is not like a virus that infects people who come into contact with it. Membership in the collective depends upon the performance of an act or the omission of an act.

Not everyone may agree with this account of collective responsibility, but suppose for the sake of argument that it is correct. Then if the members of the club committed to an ideology of racism are collectively responsible for the outcome of the racist act committed by one of its members, the contributing act of each member could be identified as the act of vice which consists in joining the club. Because someone has joined the club, this person is part of the collective that bears moral responsibility for the outcome of the racist act. Symbolic value can now be seen to be operative on two different levels. First, the act of racism symbolizes potential acts of racism by the other members. Second, each member's contributing act symbolizes potential acts of racism. The very act of joining a club committed to an ideology of racism symbolizes someone's future potential racist behavior.

This is not to say that someone's joining the club demonstrates commitment to future acts of racism, or even a propensity or readiness to commit such acts. But something is symbolic in joining a club committed to racism (in addition to being offensive in and of itself), and part of what it symbolizes is the capability to act in a racist manner, or at least having a condoning attitude toward performing such acts. Perhaps a person could be committed to racism only at the level of ideology and never on the level of overt action, and hence a person joining this club may be opposed to performing acts of racism. But even if cases such as this are possible, they do not prove that the agent's joining the club cannot symbolize his or her performing future potential acts of racism. The symbolic value of an act is determined in part by the intentions of the agent performing the act; but other factors, such as the message conveyed to others by the act, are also relevant.

In recent years Anthony Appiah and others have argued that moral agents can be tainted by the evil acts of others with whom they are connected in some significant fashion (Appiah, 1987, pp. 187ff.). A person who is tainted by such acts does not bear moral responsibility or belong to a collective which bears moral responsibility for these acts or their consequences, but Appiah argues that the person's moral integrity is nevertheless affected. Thus, a man can be tainted by the criminal acts of his brother, and a surgical nurse can be tainted by the medical malpractice of a physician whom he or she assists. While the judgment that the man bears responsibility for his brother's criminal acts or that the nurse bears moral responsibility for the physician's malpractice may be false, Appiah's point is that their moral integrity is nevertheless adversely affected.

Here my purpose is not to comment upon whether or not such a moral category as taint exists. But if such a moral category as taint is real, we may suppose that the concept of symbolic value can help explain the basis for ascribing moral taint. In the book of Joshua a man named Achan returns from a battle with possessions of those who have been captured, in spite of having been forbidden to take them. Achan returns to his tent and buries these possessions in a hole. When he is discovered to have done this, Achan is put to death. But members of his extended family are likewise put to death. While some might be inclined to raise questions about the severity of their treatment, the point of the present discussion is that if Achan's family members are tainted by his wrongdoing it is because his act symbolizes their having done the same. Although none of them returned with captured possessions, his doing it is symbolic of their having done it as well. In general, taint can take place when the act of an evildoer symbolizes a similar act by one to whom this person is connected in some significant manner.

Paul Ricoeur describes essentially this same phenomenon in a discussion of defilement. According to him, defilement is a symbol of evil. "Defilement is to stain or spot what lustration is to washing. . . .it is a symbolic stain (Ricoeur, 1967, p. 36)." If I am defiled by the stain that attaches to my criminal brother, this takes place by virtue of symbolization. The defilement that attaches to me is a symbolic stain: it is symbolic of the stain which attaches to him.

When the collective is a formal organization, such as a corporation, with established hierarchies of authority, the symbolic value of an act of virtue can be striking in its effect on the thinking of those both inside and outside the organization. The symbolic value of actions by people in positions of corporate leadership are likely to take on exaggerated significance. When corporate leaders perform acts of virtue while acting in an official capacity, these acts symbolize virtuous patterns of actions throughout the organization. Those within the organization are likely to be inspired to perform acts of virtue, and those outside the organization form impressions of the organization as a place where the virtue in question is likely to be practiced. Similar remarks apply to acts of vice performed by corporate leaders acting in an official capacity.

Those who write about applied ethics frequently talk about the importance of promoting a favorable moral climate within an organization, and I believe that the moral climate is determined, at least in part, by the symbolic value of these acts of virtue and vice. Those in positions of leadership are frequently said to set the moral tone of an organization, and what this means is that the acts of virtue or vice performed by these people are highly symbolic of a wider pattern of virtue or vice. The moral climate is constitutive of this wider pattern, and for this reason those in positions of leadership ought to consider the symbolic value of what they do when they act in the name of the organization. Traditional ethical theories have stressed the importance of acting out of good will or bringing about good consequences. But public figures should ascertain something else as well, namely, what their actions symbolize. And part of what this involves is ascertaining how these acts appear in the eyes of others.

While the symbolic value of the actions of these public figures can take on significance, their inaction can have significant symbolic value. Suppose that a senior level manager in a large corporation receives a report from a subordinate describing a decision he or she has made, and suppose the action being recommended is highly questionable as far as good ethics is concerned. The manager can exercise veto power over the recommended action but elects not to, and the decision is implemented. Here the symbolic value of the manager's inaction can be significant. It can encourage subordinates to recommend future questionable courses of action, and to others it may symbolize the willingness of the firm's leadership to overlook or condone questionable decisions within the firm.

The same phenomenon can be observed in governmental decision making. Just as the symbolic value of actions or inaction by influential persons in corporations can take on exaggerated significance, the same is sometimes true of actions of virtue or vice performed by governmental authorities. Nozick gives an example in which a decision is made whether to save a trapped miner. The symbolic value of a negative decision on the part of governmental officials for reasons of cost can be chilling in its effects. Only slightly less chilling would be the symbolic value of their taking no action at all. Clearly, public officials would do well to develop an awareness of symbolic value and take it into account when deciding upon courses of action with some measure of visibility.

Having now introduced the concept of symbolic value, I return to the discussion of moral expectation. In the remainder of this chapter I explore the notion of symbolic value as it bears upon acts that embody or manifest moral expectation. Because moral obligation is a species of moral expectation, what is said about the symbolic value of moral expectation applies to moral obligation.

Suppose that a person can be morally expected to perform a particular act, and the person in fact performs this act. If the performance of the act is witnessed by others who are aware that the person is expected to perform this act, then they are aware that the person has fulfilled a moral expectation. So far, nothing is of symbolic significance in this situation. But one person witnessing this act may go on to perceive its performance as suggestive of subsequent instances of fulfilled expectations by the person performing the act. In other words, the witness may begin to feel a type of confidence that this is an individual who is likely to fulfil his or her moral expectations. Sometimes trust has its origins in the symbolic value of someone's fulfilling a moral expectation.

In this way the performance of the act symbolizes the performance of future acts that fulfill moral expectations. If this were a prediction based upon a single instance it would be open to ridicule. But symbolic value does not derive its worth or legitimacy from a conformity to the laws of inductive reasoning. It is not predictive, and it is not in any sense the derivation of a conclusion from a body of evidence.

Consider a slightly different scenario. Suppose that person A verbalizes a moral expectation to person B. That is, A informs B that she is expected to perform a certain act, and suppose that B goes on to perform this act. The people witnessing A's verbalization of the expectation and B's carrying out the expectation know that B has fulfilled an expectation after being informed of it by A. But, as before, one witness may perceive this scenario as suggestive of a pattern of B's fulfilling future expectations verbalized by others. The symbolic value of B's act may consist in the beginnings of a confidence in B's willingness to carry out moral expectations when they are brought to her attention. If B were a child, she might begin to be thought of as a child who does what she is told.

Symbolic value can be generated by the fulfillment of a moral expectation by someone who represents others. Imagine that a visitor to a city in another part of the world approaches one of its citizens with a request for directions. This citizen can be expected to treat the visitor with civility and, assuming that the request is comprehended, the citizen can be expected to make a polite effort to provide an answer. If the citizen makes a polite effort to provide an answer, then on one level the citizen can be said to have fulfilled a moral expectation. But on another level, someone can perceive this act as suggestive of similar acts by other inhabitants of the city. Someone can begin to form the impression of these inhabitants as helpful to strangers asking directions.

Naturally, the failure to fulfil a moral expectation can reflect badly upon those whom a person represents. If the citizen does not make a polite effort to provide an answer to a visitor, then the citizen's rude behavior becomes suggestive of similar acts by other inhabitants. The impression someone forms is consequently less than favorable of the inhabitants as far as their treatment of strangers asking directions.

Sometimes the verbalization of a moral expectation takes on symbolic value. When someone informs another of a moral expectation, an impression of what is said can be formed by anyone who hears it. The verbalization may come across as wise, misguided, or insightful, depending upon what is said, to whom it is said, and under what circumstances. Suppose that the verbalization comes across to a particular observer as wise. Then the observer may find this as suggestive of wise pronouncements by this person in the future. Alternatively, the observer may find this as suggestive of wise pronouncements by others whom this person happens to represent.

The refusal to fulfil a moral expectation can symbolize a pattern of refusals. If one person verbalizes a moral expectation to another, and the second person refuses to fulfil it, an observer may form an impression of the second person as one who is likely to refuse future invitations to perform acts that fulfil moral expectations. The symbolic value of a refusal can give rise to a strong impression regarding the person who refuses. A public refusal to carry out a moral expectation verbalized by one's parent can give rise to lasting impressions by those who observe such a scene.

The situation is more complicated when a person makes a promise to fulfil a moral expectation. Unlike the acts already considered, the promise to fulfil a moral expectation creates a moral expectation. The person making the promise can be morally expected to carry out the promise. Suppose a man can be morally expected to perform a particular act, and he promises to fulfil this expectation. In some sense he now has a double moral expectation to perform the act. However, if, as appears likely, people are normally morally obligated to carry out their promises, the promise creates a moral obligation to perform the act where none previously existed. Thus, if the man ends up failing to perform the act, the failure violates duty as the result of his having made a promise.

Imagine, though, that the man carries out his promise and performs the act in question. A person who observes the man making this promise and performing this act knows that the man is carrying out his promise. Moreover, if the observer knows that the act is one that the man is morally expected to perform, the observer also knows that the man is carrying out his promise to fulfil a moral expectation. The symbolic aspects of the situation come into play when the observer sees the fulfillment of the promise as suggestive of a pattern extending into the future. The man, in other words, is perceived as one who is likely to keep his promises. In addition, the observer may perceive the man as someone who is likely to make promises or to make promises regarding his moral expectations. Moreover, if the man represents others, the symbolic value of his keeping his promise may cast them in a favorable light.

Forgetting to fulfil a moral expectation can generate symbolic value, but the situation is complicated by the fact that someone's forgetting to do something is not normally an observable state of affairs. Suppose an observer knows that a man is expected to perform an act, and the man forgets to perform it. The observer may not have enough information to know that the man has forgotten to perform the act. For all the observer knows, the man plans to perform it at a future time or has decided not to perform it. However, in some situations an observer may come to know that a person has forgotten to fulfil a moral expectation. This person's forgetfulness may then come to symbolize a pattern of forgetfulness regarding his or her moral expectations in the future.

Frequently people are mistaken about what they are morally expected to do, and as a result they fulfil the wrong moral expectation. Suppose that someone signs up to do volunteer work at a local community center, and a schedule is issued to her listing the times at which she is assigned to appear at the center. She can then be expected to appear at the center at the times indicated. If she loses the schedule and appears in the afternoon on a day when she is assigned to appear in the morning, then she could be said to have fulfilled the wrong moral expectation. To staff members at the community center who realize that she is mistaken about her assignment this may come to symbolize a pattern of confusion regarding her assignments reaching into the future. The symbolic value of fulfilling the wrong moral expectation can lead others to question their confidence in an individual's ability to identify the moral expectation that needs to be fulfilled.

In each of the examples so far presented the symbolic value of the action has been described from the perspective of those observing the action and the circumstances of its performance. In each example the performance of the action could be perceived by these observers as suggestive of a pattern extending into the future. However, symbolic value can likewise be generated in the absence of other persons. The person performing the action is capable of apprehending or recognizing the possibility or likelihood of patterns consisting of his or her own actions extending into the future. Hence someone can sense the symbolic value of his or her own actions.

Recall the example from the opening chapter in which someone is standing near a store's entrance waiting for the rain to subside while a woman carrying packages is struggling to open the doors. Suppose that this person almost without thinking reaches for the door and opens it for the woman. This person may subsequently reflect upon the situation and realize that she carried out a moral expectation, and this realization may lead her to see this fulfilled expectation as suggestive of a pattern of future potential actions. For example, the action may symbolize to her that she is the sort of person who will jump to the aid of people, even total strangers, unless perhaps the act requires a great deal of sacrifice on her part. Likewise, the act may symbolize to her that she is the sort of person who will come to the aid of others without even thinking about the situation. Through reflecting upon the symbolic value of their actions, people can come to learn a great deal about themselves.

To summarize, the notion of symbolic value, derived from Robert Nozick's notion of symbolic utility, involves the idea that the performance of one act can symbolize the actual or potential performances of other acts in a manner which has moral significance. Sometimes this phenomenon takes place in the context of conventions that are in effect, and sometimes it takes place in the absence of conventions. The symbolic value is determined in part by the agent's intent in performing the act in question, but it is also determined in part by the perception of the act by others. When the agent is in a position of leadership, the symbolic value of the agent's action can take on an enlarged significance. Within a formal organization the symbolic value of the actions of its leaders can help set the moral tone of the organization.

The symbolic value of fulfilling a moral expectation can be revealed in a feeling that the person performing the relevant act is likely to fulfil moral expectations in the future. This feeling can give rise to the beginnings of a feeling of confidence or trust. It is not intended as a prediction based on evidence, but it does point to the future and can have significance as far as what others feel about the person. The fulfillment of a moral expectation by a person who represents others can be suggestive of similar acts by those who are represented by the person. Because of the symbolic value of this act, the act can reflect either positively or negatively upon the others.

The act of verbalizing a moral expectation can itself take on symbolic value. If the verbalization comes across as wise, it may symbolize to others wise pronouncements by the same person in the future. The refusal to carry out a moral expectation is a pronouncement that may be suggestive of a pattern of refusing future invitations to perform acts that fulfill moral expectations. The symbolic value of a promise to fulfil a moral expectation together with the subsequent fulfillment of this promise may be revealed in the perception that the person is likely to keep future promises. If an observer knows that a person has forgotten to fulfil a moral expectation, the person's act of forgetting may come to symbolize a pattern of forgetfulness in carrying out moral expectations in the future. And carrying out the wrong moral expectation may come to symbolize a pattern of confusion about identifying someone's moral expectations. Finally, symbolic value can be generated in the absence of others. In many situations a person can sense the symbolic value of his or her own actions.

Nine

OFFENCE AND EXPECTATION

An act of offence is standardly characterized as an act whose performance is morally blameworthy and whose omission is neither morally praiseworthy nor the fulfillment of moral duty. Thus, performing an act of offence is morally blameworthy but stops short of constituting the violation of moral duty, and nothing is praiseworthy in refraining from the act. Roderick Chisholm calls attention to these acts in his 1963 article, "Supererogation and Offence: A Conceptual Scheme for Ethics,"'nd in this article they are first referred to as acts of offence.

Chisholm describes the category of offence as a kind of "complement" to the category of supererogation (Chisholm, 1963, p. 2). Just as acts of supererogation are praiseworthy to perform, acts of offence are blameworthy to perform. Moreover, just as acts of supererogation are not obligatory to perform, acts of offence are not obligatory to omit. And just as acts of supererogation are not blameworthy to omit, acts of offence are not praiseworthy to omit. Chisholm appears to have become aware of the category of offence as something of a logical complement to the category of supererogation, and he urges that an ethical system that provides a place for supererogation should also provide a place for offence.

In this chapter I survey what some philosophers say about acts of offence and acts of other closely related types, and I believe that doing so will lead to a better understanding of moral expectation. For if a person maintains, as I have done in earlier chapters, that the category of moral expectation is not exhausted by moral duty, then the person is almost certain to acknowledge the possibility of offence. Suppose that someone acknowledges the possibility that an act we are morally expected to perform is not our moral duty to perform. Then the omission of this act is both morally blameworthy and not morally obligatory to omit. Thus, acknowledging a non-obligatory act that we are expected to perform entails acknowledging an act (its omission) which is both blameworthy and non-obligatory to omit. If we acknowledge in addition that such acts can fail to be praiseworthy to omit, we acknowledge that acts of offence are possible.

In simpler terms, the failure to carry out a non-obligatory moral expectation which attaches to us is an offence in cases where fulfilling the expectation is not morally praiseworthy. Because rarely is anything morally praiseworthy in carrying out our moral expectations, we might regard the final clause as superfluous for all practical purposes. This is not to say that all offences can be construed as the failure to carry out moral expectations. But the failure to carry out a non-obligatory moral expectation can for all practical purposes be identified as an offence. In this way an examination of moral offence can help shed some light on the failure to carry out our moral expectations.

An example of an act of offence provided by Chisholm in an article co-authored by Ernest Sosa is taking too long in a restaurant when others are known to be waiting for tables. If a person is lingering at his or her table after having finished a meal with the awareness that others are waiting, then Chisholm and Sosa believe that the person's lingering constitutes an offence. Although the person is violating no moral duty, this behavior is nevertheless morally blameworthy and nothing is morally praiseworthy in refraining from lingering.

If Chisholm and Sosa are correct in identifying this act as an act of offence, then, although no one has a moral duty to perform it, a person can arguably be morally expected to do so. People who have finished their meal and are aware of others waiting for tables are not morally obliged to leave their table, but they are open to moral blame if they take too long in departing. Perhaps the degree to which they are blameworthy is relatively insignificant, but under the circumstances they can be expected not to linger. Refraining from lingering in this situation is a matter of common courtesy.

In many types of situations refraining from an act of offence can be described as an act of common courtesy, and often such refraining is at the same time the fulfillment of moral expectation. Acts of common courtesy are frequently acts which people can reasonably be expected to perform. At the same time, they are rarely acts which people have a moral obligation to perform. Failing to perform an act of common courtesy is blameworthy but not the violation of duty.

Julia Driver argues in favor of a category of acts she refers to as "the suberogatory." Suberogatory acts are characterized by Driver as acts that are bad to perform but not forbidden. They are "acts which are worse than the situation calls for, but *not* forbidden (Driver, 1992, p. 286)." Elsewhere she characterizes these acts as "permissible, though bad (*Ibid.*, p. 291)." They are morally permissible in the sense of not being morally forbidden, and what this means is that performing them does not violate moral duty.

In referring to suberogatory acts as "bad" Driver appears to mean that they are open to moral blame. She describes an example in which passengers are boarding a crowded train, a couple wish to sit together, and in only one place are two unoccupied seats next to one another. A man entering the train just ahead of the couple knows that they wish to sit together, and that he could take a less convenient seat for himself. Driver believes that for him to take one of the two adjacent unoccupied seats would be blameworthy. If he refuses to take a less convenient seat, then he has done something bad for which he can be blamed (*Ibid.* p. 289).

The relationship between suberogatory acts and acts of offence appears to be the following. Both are morally blameworthy to perform, and neither is morally obligatory to omit. But while acts of offence are not praiseworthy to omit,

Driver leaves open the possibility that suberogatory acts are praiseworthy to omit. In fact, she believes that for the man entering the train ahead of the couple to take a less convenient seat for himself would be praiseworthy. If so, his taking the blameworthy course of action, sitting in one of the adjacent seats, does not qualify as an act of offence.

Driver points out that what she calls suberogatory acts, although still obscure and almost entirely unknown, have actually been long recognized in some Islamic codes of ethics. One such code divides actions into five basic moral categories: the required, the forbidden, the recommended, the discouraged, and the permitted. Driver notes that the category of the recommended roughly corresponds to supererogation, and the category of the discouraged roughly corresponds to the suberogatory.

Suberogatory acts are morally permissible, and hence they might also seem to correspond to the fifth category, the permitted. However, I believe that the fifth category should be taken to comprise only those permitted acts that fail to fall into previous categories (such acts are described by Chisholm as belonging to the category of the "neutral"). They are permitted acts that are to be classified no with the recommended nor with the discouraged. An example of such an act might be a man's absentmindedly scratching his nose.

By distinguishing between the category of the forbidden and that of the discouraged, this code of ethics opens the door to acts which are morally bad or substandard but not forbidden. An act someone is morally discouraged from performing is presumably an act which is open to moral blame or criticism in some fashion. Given that such an act is explicitly distinguished from the category of the forbidden, Driver's contention that this category corresponds roughly to that of the suberogatory is plausible.

The category of the discouraged roughly corresponds to the failure of non-obligatory moral expectation. When someone has a moral expectation to perform an act and lacks a moral obligation to perform the act, then omitting to perform the act can be described as something to be discouraged. Someone can be morally discouraged from failing to carry out such moral expectations.

Michael J. Zimmerman does not argue in favor of suberogatory acts as such, and indeed he is not convinced that they are possible. However, he sets out to refute the principle that a person is morally blameworthy for performing an act only if the person has a moral obligation not to perform the act. He refers to this principle as (B2). Thus, he affirms the principle that a person can be morally blameworthy for performing an act without having a moral obligation to omit the act. From this principle to the principle that the performance of a person's act can be blameworthy without being obligatory to omit is a short step. But because Zimmerman draws a sharp distinction between the claim that a person is blameworthy for performing an act and the claim that the act performed by the person is blameworthy, he is not convinced that the latter principle can be inferred from the former principle.

Nevertheless, Zimmerman's work is relevant to the present discussion for two reasons. First, those who are not inclined to draw a sharp distinction between the blame which is attributed to an agent for performing an act and the blame which is attributed to the act itself can regard his arguments as promoting the cause for suberogatory acts. Suppose a moral agent is blameworthy for performing a particular act. Then the performance of the act is the reason for the agent's being blameworthy, and many will find that this plausibly entails that something is blameworthy in the performance of the act as well (though what is blameworthy about the person need not be the same as what is blameworthy about the performance). But if the performance of the act can be blameworthy without being obligatory to omit, the performance qualifies as suberogatory even if the act itself does not.

Second, even if someone believes that a moral agent can be blameworthy for performing an act without anything being blameworthy in what the agent does, a person who sets out to refute (B2) is embracing a position at least very much in the spirit of what Chisholm, Sosa, and Driver affirm. For someone who denies (B2) is committed to holding that a moral agent can be morally blameworthy for performing an act without having a moral obligation to omit the act. Now whether or not the act or its performance is itself blameworthy, the performance of the act is the sole reason for the agent's being blameworthy. Thus, although the act is not itself blameworthy, it has the causal power to render the agent blameworthy. And if we affirm that the agent is not obligated to omit any such act, the agent is morally permitted to perform an act which *renders* the agent morally blameworthy. Surely this position is in the neighborhood of what Chisholm, Sosa, and Driver argue.

Another way to state this point is to observe that those who oppose the possibility of suberogatory acts will be unlikely to find Zimmerman's position attractive. Typically those who oppose the possibility of suberogatory acts are motivated by the intuition that nothing blameworthy falls outside the boundaries of what is obligatory to omit. And someone motivated by this intuition will hardly accept the idea that an agent can be blameworthy for doing something without having an obligation to omit doing it. Why a person would not find this idea repugnant, in other words, is hard to see if the idea of a blameworthy but permissible act strikes the person as repugnant.

Zimmerman's concern in refuting this principle is to block an argument by David Widerker which purports to show that the ought implies can principle entails the controversial and much discussed principle of alternate possibilities (or at least the portion of this principle which deals with moral blame: A person is morally blameworthy for performing an act only if not to perform the act is within the person's power). Harry Frankfurt, who is well known for his arguments against the principle of alternate possibilities, insists that his arguments do not refute the ought implies can principle. But Widerker correctly shows that (B2), which he claims to be a necessary truth, allows one to derive the principle of alternate possibilities from the ought implies can principle (Widerker, 1991, p. 223). Thus, with the aid of (B2), Frankfurt's arguments against the principle of alternate possibilities apply equally to the ought implies can principle.

Zimmerman comes to Frankfurt's defense in arguing that (B2) is false. His case against this principle is based on his observation that sometimes agents perform acts they falsely believe they are not morally justified in performing. Thus, even though they are in fact justified in performing the acts in question, they believe that this is not so. Zimmerman contends that an agent is morally blameworthy for performing such an act. To do that which we believe we are not justified in doing is morally blameworthy. But acts of this type are at the same time morally permissible. If an agent is justified in performing an act, the performance of the act is not the violation of moral duty. Zimmerman concludes that agents are sometimes morally blameworthy for performing such acts without being morally obliged not to perform them (Zimmerman, 1993, p. 52). And if any such acts exist, principle (B2) is false.

Widerker replies to Zimmerman in an article co-authored with Charlotte Katzoff. They take exception to Zimmerman's own principle that an agent is morally blameworthy for performing an act if the agent believes that he has a moral obligation not to perform the act. Widerker and Katzoff provide three examples they take to be counter-examples to this principle (Widerker and Katzoff, 1994, p. 286). In the first a Nazi soldier believes he has a moral obligation to exterminate Jews and not to spare their life. One day he saves the life of a Jewish child, an act that makes him morally blameworthy according to Zimmerman's principle. The authors believe otherwise; they cannot understand how saving a child's life can render him morally blameworthy.

In the second example a demon endows someone with an irresistible desire to strangle a neighbor's canary. The person is unaware of this fact and believes she is obliged to refrain from this act. If she proceeds to strangle the canary, she is classified as morally blameworthy by Zimmerman's principle. But the authors believe she cannot be judged her morally blameworthy, since she is acting from an irresistible impulse.

The third example involves a physician who believes that a particular drug is the only way to alleviate a patient's suffering. The physician believes that he has a moral obligation not to let the patient suffer, but inexplicably ignores this obligation in favor of watching a football game. However, the drug is in fact unavailable to the physician, a fact he does not realize. Here too the authors believe that to judge the agent morally blameworthy would be wrong, contrary to the verdict Zimmerman's principle yields. To judge the physician blameworthy for the omission when he is unable to do otherwise would be unreasonable.

Although we might not be convinced by all of these examples, we might well agree with Widerker and Katzoff that Zimmerman's principle admits of counter-examples. We are not always morally blameworthy for performing an act we believe we have a moral obligation not to perform. Curiously, the authors do not address the issue of whether someone is ever morally blameworthy for performing such an act. For if any such acts exist, and if Zimmerman is correct that such acts can be permissible to perform, then principle (B2) is false.

Zimmerman appeals to a universal principle in setting out to show that principle (B2) is false. The principle, if true, would indeed show that (B2) is false. Widerker and Katzoff reply to Zimmerman by arguing that this universal principle admits of counter-examples, and I am inclined to think that in this they are correct. But they show no evident concern that (B2) is likewise refuted if the principle has any true instantiations whatsoever. If a person is ever blameworthy for doing what he or she falsely believes is morally unjustified, thereby doing what is morally permissible, then principle (B2) is refuted.

This point is addressed in Zimmerman's 1997 article, "A Plea for Accuses." The title of this article is intended to evoke memories of J.L. Austin's famous paper, "A Plea for Excuses," and Zimmerman wishes to introduce the notion of an accuse as an analogue to the notion of an excuse. Since the publication of Austin's paper in 1957, the distinction between a justification and an excuse has been widely recognized as follows. A person has a justification for an action just in case the person did not do wrong in performing it. A person has an excuse for an action, on the other hand, just in case the person did do wrong in performing it but is not blameworthy for having performed it.

The work of Austin has helped make clear that wrongdoing and blame are separable. When a person has an excuse for doing something morally wrong, the person is not morally blameworthy for doing so. In other words, morally wrong behavior is compatible with the absence of moral blame.

Zimmerman argues that the presence of moral blame is compatible with the absence of morally wrong behavior. Sometimes a person who does nothing morally wrong nevertheless does something for which he or she is morally blameworthy. Zimmerman coins the term "accuse" to refer to the reasons or grounds for imputing blameworthiness in these circumstances. Just as an excuse constitutes the grounds for not imputing blameworthiness despite the presence of wrongdoing, an accuse refers to the grounds for imputing blameworthiness despite the absence of wrongdoing.

If Zimmerman is correct that accuses exist, then principle (B2) is refuted. Suppose an accuse exists for an act which a person performs. Then by the definition of an accuse nothing is morally wrong in the performance of the act. So the act does not violate moral duty, for to think that nothing is morally wrong in the violation of moral duty is inconceivable. By the definition of an accuse the person is also morally blameworthy for performing the act. Hence the performance of the act renders the person morally blameworthy without violating moral duty, and this contradicts (B2).

To suppose that an agent can be morally blameworthy for doing something involving no moral wrongdoing might be initially puzzling. Zimmerman dispels this puzzle in two stages. First, he establishes a distinction between doing objective moral wrong and believing that we are doing objective moral wrong. Second, he argues that sometimes a person is morally blameworthy for acting in the belief that he or she is doing objective moral wrong. These two facts open the door to the possibility that someone who acts in the belief that he or she is doing objective moral wrong is blameworthy for doing so in spite of not doing anything which involves objective moral wrong. And this opens the door to the possibility of accuses.

Zimmerman distinguishes two groups of cases. The first group consists of cases where a person who is acting freely believes that he or she is doing objective moral wrong but is not morally blameworthy. In the second group are cases where a person who is acting freely believes that he or she is doing objective moral wrong, he or she is blameworthy for doing so, and is in fact doing moral wrong. Zimmerman observes that if all pertinent cases fall into one or the other of these groups, then his argument for accuses fails.

His strategy is to select examples which appear to fall into each group and show that upon closer inspection they are examples in which accuses are present (Zimmerman, 1997, pp. 235–236). One example involves Sarah who has overly demanding moral standards. She is a saintly person who believes that her duty is to exhaust herself in the service of others, whereas she is actually behaving in a supererogatory manner. One day she is awakened by her alarm but collapses into bed and sleeps for an extra hour. She feels guilty for having done so, because she believes this is the wrong thing to do.

Although we may be tempted to regard Sarah as having done nothing to render her blameworthy and hence having done something which falls into the first group of cases, Zimmerman argues at length that this is not so. Sarah is admirable in many respects, and she has given of herself for others. But she is blameworthy to at least a minimal degree for having deliberately chosen what she regards as the violation of moral duty. This is not to say that others are justified in expressing blame to Sarah for her actions; this is only to say that she is blameworthy.

An example that might appear to fall into the second group involves Dan, a small child, who is in some type of danger. Paul picks up Dan and rescues him from danger by running off with him. However, Paul does not realize that Dan is in danger; in fact, Paul's motive is to upset Dan. But Dan, far from being upset, is quite relieved to be rescued from danger.

In this example Paul might appear to commit moral wrongdoing and be blameworthy for acting as he does. Zimmerman concurs in regarding Paul as blameworthy since Paul believes he is acting wrongly, but he argues convincingly that Paul does not in fact commit wrong. Although Paul attempts wrongdoing he actually rescues Dan from danger, and this appears to be the right thing to do under the circumstances. Zimmerman leaves open the possibility that Paul does something that is morally "untoward," but he denies that Paul does wrong. In the end Paul's grounds for acting can be identified as an accuse (*Ibid.*, p. 237).

Zimmerman concludes that the possibility of accuses is confirmed rather than refuted by considering examples such as these. In each example he concludes that the agent is morally blameworthy but commits no objective moral wrong. Sarah is morally blameworthy for acting in the belief that she is violating moral duty, and Paul is morally blameworthy for acting in the belief that he is upsetting Dan. But neither Sarah nor Paul does anything that qualifies as objective moral wrong. Again, these are examples that might initially appear not to involve accuses. And while we might have difficulty in seeing these peripheral cases as examples of accuses, plenty of ordinary cases can be found where no objective moral wrongdoing takes place and yet the agent incurs moral blame for acting in the mistaken belief that he or she is committing wrong.

The upshot of this discussion is that principle (B2) is false. A person can incur moral blame for an act the person has no moral obligation to omit. Accordingly, Widerker's argument that from the ought implies can principle the principle of alternate possibilities can be deduced fails. Widerker's argument succeeds only if principle (B2) is true, and Zimmerman's case for accuses suffices to show that principle (B2) is false.

To summarize, Chisholm and Sosa's acts of offence are morally blameworthy to perform and neither morally obligatory nor praiseworthy to omit. Driver's suberogatory acts are the same, except that the possibility is left open that a suberogatory act is praiseworthy to omit. In addition, suberogatory acts are similar to acts falling into the category of the discouraged in some Islamic codes of ethics. Zimmerman's affirmation of acts that render an agent morally blameworthy without being morally obligatory to omit comes by way of rejecting Widerker's principle that such acts are impossible. Such acts arise, according to Zimmerman, when an agent acts in the mistaken belief that he or she is doing that that constitutes the violation of moral duty. Zimmerman defines an accuse as the reason or grounds for imputing blameworthiness despite the absence of wrongdoing. He introduces this notion as the moral analogue of an excuse. Clearly the presence of an accuse signals the presence of an act which is morally blameworthy to perform but not morally obligatory to omit.

In the remainder of this chapter I draw together some of the themes from the foregoing survey and discuss their relevance to the notion of moral expectation. What all of the authors so far presented have in common is the conviction that an act can be morally blameworthy (or render an agent morally blameworthy) without crossing the line which separates permissibility from the violation of moral obligation. An act which violates moral obligation is obviously morally blameworthy, assuming no excuse is present, but what these authors contend is that some blameworthy acts (or acts which render agents blameworthy) go beyond the realm of violating moral duty. Thus, the performance of an act can be morally objectionable to the extent that it is worthy of moral blame or causes a person to be blameworthy but not so objectionable that it violates moral duty.

Not everyone will agree that such acts are possible. Some have expressed the opinion that an act whose performance is bad enough to be morally blameworthy is not permitted. How, people sometimes ask, can a moral agent be morally permitted to do that which is blameworthy? Or someone might put the matter is somewhat different terms by wondering how anything can be morally blameworthy in doing that which is morally permissible.

Some reject the possibility that moral agents can perform acts of supererogation on the grounds that no matter how praiseworthy our actions are, we are simply carrying out our moral duty. We can never go above and beyond the call of duty by acting in a morally praiseworthy manner. Those who reject the possibility that morally praiseworthy acts can go beyond the scope of moral duty are likely to argue that no morally blameworthy acts can go beyond the scope of the moral duty to refrain. In other words, if a person believes that the realm of moral obligation is vast enough to swallow up all that is morally praiseworthy, the person is likely to believe that the realm of the morally forbidden is vast enough to swallow up all that is morally blameworthy. Someone who subscribes to a strict and demanding view of moral obligation is likely to subscribe to a strict and demanding view of the morally forbidden.

The logical connection between these issues and moral expectation is straightforward. All of the writers surveyed in this chapter are agreed that an act can be morally blameworthy (or render an agent blameworthy) without violating moral duty. For the sake of simplicity I will refer to them using Driver's designation of the suberogatory. If what we are morally expected to do is always morally blameworthy to fail to carry out, then the failure to carry out a moral expectation is a suberogatory act unless the moral expectation is at the same time a moral duty. Thus, the relationship between morally expected acts and suberogatory acts is that the failure to carry out our moral expectation when it is not our moral duty is a suberogatory act (this characterization depends upon construing omissions of acts as acts in their own right; those who are averse to construing omissions in this manner may prefer an alternate characterization).

From this we cannot deduce that the failure to perform a suberogatory act is an act someone is morally expected to perform. In other words, someone cannot always be expected to refrain from suberogatory acts. One reason is that suberogatory acts can be morally praiseworthy to omit, and seldom if ever is carrying out one's moral expectations morally praiseworthy. Driver discusses morally "charged" situations in which the same act can be praiseworthy to perform and blameworthy to omit or blameworthy to perform and praiseworthy to omit, and she believes that some acts falling into the latter category are suberogatory. I am inclined to think that she is correct regarding this matter, but the proposition that we are morally expected to refrain from all such suberogatory acts is far from evident.

Recall that acts of offence differ from suberogatory acts in that to omit an act of offence is never morally praiseworthy. Thus, unless we are in a situation where carrying out our moral expectation is praiseworthy, the failure to carry out our moral expectation qualifies as an offence. Can we always be morally expected to refrain from an offence? Here the situation is no longer complicated by the presence of an suberogatory acts which are praiseworthy to omit, for acts of offence are never praiseworthy to omit. Accordingly, to assert that moral agents can always be expected to refrain from acts of offence may seem reasonable.

Nevertheless, I am not convinced that this is the case. Consider an act whose performance is morally blameworthy to only a minimal degree. Is the proposition that someone is morally expected to refrain from it a foregone conclusion? In the absence of reasons for supposing it is true, an affirmative answer is not clear. That someone could correctly expect me to refrain from an act whose performance is only barely blameworthy is not evident.

What does seem evident is that some will refuse to acknowledge that moral expectation can embrace acts that are not morally obligatory. Those who subscribe to a strict and demanding view of the morally forbidden will be among this group. For if someone has a moral expectation that is not morally obligatory, then the failure to carry it out qualifies as an offence. But if a person subscribes to a strict and demanding view of the morally forbidden, then the person will not acknowledge the possibility of an offence. And if offences are not possible, then someone cannot fail to carry out a moral expectation that is not morally obligatory. But since a moral expectation which moral agents cannot fail (in the logical sense of "cannot") to carry out is not possible, no such moral expectation is possible.

The last step of this argument requires a closer look. Suppose that someone cannot fail to carry out a moral expectation that is not morally obligatory. This proposition can be interpreted as the claim that in no possible world does an agent have a moral expectation which is not morally obligatory where the agent fails to carry it out. Given this fact, can possible worlds exist in which the agent has a moral expectation that is not obligatory? If this were true, then in every one of these worlds the agent carries out the moral expectation. In other words, the fact that such expectations are carried out is a necessary truth. But no moral expectations are carried out in all possible worlds. Hence, given the initial supposition, no possible world exists in which a moral expectation is not obligatory. To reiterate, if offences are not possible, then no moral expectation can fail to be morally obligatory.

Identifying offence as the failure of moral expectation when it is not morally obligatory can help shed some light on the nature of moral obligation. Here Zimmerman's remarks are illuminating. According to Zimmerman, a judgment of blameworthiness is, "Not a judgment of the person *in toto*; rather, it is a judgment of the person with respect to a certain episode in or aspect of his or her life. A person who is blameworthy in the present sense is blameworthy *for* something, some *particular* thing. . . .This thing, whatever it is, reflects ill on the person, and the person's moral standing is thus diminished to that extent (*Ibid.*, p. 230)."

A person who is morally blameworthy for some particular thing experiences a diminished moral standing, and this is true even if the person does not violate moral duty. An important lesson to be learned from this point is that the successful avoidance of the morally forbidden does not ensure a high moral standing. A man who strictly devotes his life to ensuring that he violates no moral obligation is to be commended, but the person is mistaken if he thinks that this formula is enough to guarantee a high moral standing. Elsewhere I have referred to this approach to the moral life as a type of modern day Phariseeism (Mellema, 1991, p. 200). The work of Chisholm, Sosa, Driver, and Zimmerman helps to reveal the weakness inherent in this approach to the moral life. It is a failure to see that moral blame is independent of moral duty and that a strict adherence to moral duty is not enough to achieve a high moral standing. We must take the additional step of avoiding what is morally blameworthy.

Taking this additional step, I submit, leads us to acknowledge that we have moral expectations over and above moral obligation. A failure to take these expectations seriously places us in the position where our moral standing can be diminished. Ignoring these moral expectations has consequences, and we should be cautious about dismissing these consequences as trivial and insignificant. The work of Chisholm, Sosa, Driver, and Zimmerman helps place this matter in perspective and makes possible a deep appreciation of what is involved in failing to take our moral expectations seriously.

Islamic codes of ethics recognize a distinction between the forbidden and the discouraged, and a growing awareness among contemporary moralists of the importance of this distinction appears to exist. We need to acknowledge acts which morality discourages us from performing over and above what we are morally forbidden from performing. As Zimmerman points out, these acts reflect ill on those who perform them. Just as the failure to take this point seriously can produce a distorted picture of the moral life, my conviction is that taking this point seriously can help avoid a distorted picture of moral expectation.

Ten

DIVINE EXPECTATION

Those who believe that morality is grounded upon the will of a divine being almost invariably focus upon the commandments of this divine being. In recent years, for example, the Divine Command theory of morality has been defended by several prominent philosophers. According to this view, roughly speaking, the commandments of God are what determine right and wrong. Many have attacked and challenged this view for a variety of reasons. But seldom if ever is it attacked on the grounds that it places too much emphasis upon God's commandments, as opposed to other expressions of God's will.

My suggestion in this chapter is that views that focus exclusively on the commandments of a divine being are unreasonably restrictive. Naturally, the remedy I suggest is to concentrate attention upon the expectations of a divine being (for purposes of simplicity I will speak of this being as God for the remainder of the discussion). To the extent that a person believes that morality is grounded upon, or at least partially determined by, the will of God, the person can sensibly say that God forms expectations about how we live our lives and that these expectations play a role in determining the moral status of human behavior.

Some expectations God forms about the behavior of moral agents take the form of commands. We need not deny that morality is shaped by the commands of God. Rather, God's will regarding the behavior of human moral agents goes beyond what he commands regarding their behavior. Moral expectations that do not take the form of commands can also be an expression of his will.

If a person maintains that morality is grounded upon or in any way shaped by the will of God, then the person ought to take into account the expectations of God in addition to the commands of God. Concentrating exclusively upon the commands of God yields an account that is too limited. For when God commands human beings to perform certain acts, they are morally obligated to perform these acts. Human beings are presumably not morally permitted to disobey the commands of God. But someone might also judge that acting contrary to God's will is sometimes morally blameworthy without qualifying as the violation of moral duty.

In previous chapters I have developed the idea that moral expectation is not confined to moral obligation. We can be morally expected to perform an act that we have no moral obligation to perform. Thus, someone might rightly form an expectation about another person, where the failure to carry out the expectation does not constitute the violation of moral duty. In this chapter I will discuss the possibility of God's forming such expectations. Just as human beings can form moral expectations that do not involve moral obligation on the part of the person to whom the expectation attaches, the same is true of God. God is capable of forming expectations concerning human beings that do not involve moral obligation on their part. And because the commands of God have the force of moral obligation, these expectations are independent of God's commands.

This chapter begins with a discussion of the scholastic view concerning the manner in which God reveals his will regarding the behavior of human beings. Specifically, I will address the scholastic distinction between the commands of God and the counsels of God. A moral theory that makes room for the counsels of God captures the spirit of the Islamic category of the recommended, and I will argue that the further inclusion of God's moral expectations provides the resources for capturing the category of the discouraged. After having made a case for the inclusion of moral expectations that do not carry the force of commands, I turn to the consideration of opposing views. The second half of this chapter begins with a brief survey of some leading figures of the Protestant Reformation. Although they do not explicitly address the issue of moral expectation, I urge that an acknowledgement of non-obligatory moral expectation on God's part does not fit their view regarding the nature of God. The chapter concludes with a discussion of some contemporary theists whose views preclude God's forming such expectations regarding the behavior of human beings.

A good deal of historical precedent can be found for the view that God expresses his will in ways other than commands. The scholastics held, for example, that the commandments of God can be distinguished from the counsels of God. St. Thomas Aquinas' explanation of this distinction is that a commandment of God implies obligation, while a counsel of God is optional. When God counsels someone to perform an act, whether or not to perform the act is optional for the person. God's commands, on the other hand, are never optional.

Thomas speaks of the Old Law and the New Law and characterizes the Old Law, which he refers to as the law of bondage, as composed exclusively of God's commands. The New Law, on the other hand, is the law of liberty in which God's counsels are added to God's commands (*S.T.*, Ia IIae, 108, Art. 4). A person can appropriately exercise liberty when confronted with a counsel of God. Unlike our response to a command, our responding to God's counsels with a spirit of liberty is fitting.

God's counsels are intended to benefit those who carry them out, according to Thomas. He describes them as supremely useful to those to whom God directs them, and hence responding positively is in their best interests. People are at liberty to carry them out or to decline to do so, but declining appears to be the more foolish course of action. Someone who declines is not acting in his or her best interests.

Thomas believes that the counsels of God are directed to people in the areas of their lives that relate to wealth, carnal pleasures, and honors. God counsels us to renounce wealth, carnal pleasures, and pride. If we do so entirely, we will lead a life of poverty, chastity, and obedience. We are not required to lead such a life, but the more we renounce wealth, carnal pleasures, and pride, the more we are acting in our own best interests. He states that we can attain to eternal happiness without renouncing them altogether, but the more we renounce them, the more speedily we attain eternal happiness.

Generally speaking, the counsels of God are optional recommendations, and they are intended to bring benefits to those who honor them. Thomas emphasizes that counsels are directed to people in the context of the particular circumstances of their lives, and he makes certain qualifications. Some are unfit to carry out certain counsels, and doing so is not in their best interests. But, all things considered, counsels are for our own good to carry out.

Counsels are not the same as expectations. Both are optional in that their non-performance does not violate moral duty. But no indication can be found that the non-performance of counsels is morally blameworthy. In certain instances an agent's omission to carry out a counsel of God may conceivably be blameworthy to at least a minimal degree. But to decline to carry out a counsel of God is not always blameworthy. We are certainly not blameworthy in declining to live a life of poverty or declining to live a life of chastity. Thus, counsels, unlike moral expectations, are not in general morally blameworthy to omit.

In the previous chapter the category of the discouraged in some Islamic codes of ethics was compared to the category consisting of the non-performance of acts that a person is morally expected to perform. When a person is morally expected to perform a particular act, the non-performance of this act is something which morality can be said to discourage. The scholastic notion of a counsel, on the other hand, can perhaps be compared with the category of the recommended in these Islamic codes of ethics. Acts that are recommended are distinguished from acts that are required, and hence a person has no moral obligation to perform them. At the same time, they are distinguished from acts that are (merely) permitted. To perform them is good, someone is not required to perform them, and nothing is wrong with their non-performance.

The significance of the scholastic distinction for a discussion of God's expectations is that it highlights the role of human liberty in responding to expressions of God's will. If the expression of God's will for human beings involved nothing more than commands, no room could be found for that which is optional in the responses of human beings. A command of God directed at human beings prescribes moral obligations that are binding upon them; humans are morally required to carry out that which is commanded of them by God. Humans have the ability to disobey the commands of God, but this is not liberty of the type referred to by Thomas. Liberty from the commands of God is not achieved by disobeying the commands of God. The liberty spoken of here involves the ability to decline without the threat of penalty.

A system of moral law composed exclusively of commands Thomas refers to as the law of bondage. No room can be found for the exercise of human liberty. A system of moral law that includes counsels and commands Thomas calls the law of liberty. Human beings are given the liberty free of the threat of penalty to decide whether or not to carry out the counsels. They are encouraged to carry them out, and to carry them out is in their best interests. But they are free to decline.

A system of moral law that includes both the commands of God and the counsels of God does not entail that God forms moral expectations of human beings which are not morally obligatory. But it provides a key ingredient for the possibility of such expectations, and that is the presence of human liberty in responding to expressions of God's will. It accommodates the idea that God values the freedom of choice that human beings possess. Some expressions of his will are in the form of commands, and obedience to these is morally obligatory. But counsels are expressions of his will designed to elicit choices which are conducive to human well being.

Still, more is needed in this system of moral law. If the scholastic notion of a counsel falls under the category of the recommended in the Islamic codes of ethics discussed earlier, nothing in this system of law falls under the category of the discouraged. The counsels of God embody that which God encourages human beings to do, but nothing in the system so far described captures that which God discourages human beings from doing.

Those who are convinced that the commands of God are the only expressions of his will relevant to the lives of human beings would see no value in developing a theory which includes the resources for speaking about behavior which he either encourages or discourages. But if the theory contains the resources for speaking about that which he encourages, including the resources for speaking about what he discourages human beings from doing is sensible. If God has reason to encourage human beings in the direction of certain types of behavior, he presumably has reason to discourage human beings from engaging in other types of behavior. And a theory that accommodates both his encouragement and discouragement is arguably more desirable than a theory which accommodates only the former.

Expanding a moral system to accommodate God's discouragement of certain types of behavior can be approached in two ways. One approach consists in providing an account of the positive expression of God's will in which the omission of the specified behavior is something which is discouraged. This is the approach I embrace. According to this approach, human beings are discouraged from omitting to do what God morally expects but does not command them to do.

An alternative approach would be to focus directly upon behavior God discourages. Perhaps such an approach would involve developing an account of demeritorious behavior on the part of human beings. Just as those who perform morally praiseworthy but non-obligatory acts are said to do that which is meritorious, those who perform morally blameworthy but permissible acts can be described as doing that which is demeritorious. And just as saintly persons are sometimes described as building up a treasury of merit as a result of the surplus of the good or the praiseworthy produced by their actions, persons who are prone to doing that which God discourages can perhaps be said to build up a "treasury" of demerit over the course of time. Alternatively, this type of moral theory could involve the assignment of merits and demerits to human moral agents on the basis of what they do or neglect to do.

The approach I favor identifies that which God discourages us from doing with the failure to do what he morally expects us to do but does not demand that we do. When God discourages a certain type of action, he expects people to refrain from this action. And when God discourages the omission of a certain type of action, he expects people to perform this action.

An approach strictly limited to the commands of God that has no acknowledgement of what God recommends or discourages (apart from what he commands) encourages the idea of God as a stern disciplinarian. On such an approach God expresses his will in the form of commands, one of his paramount concerns is that human beings obey these commands, and he punishes those who violate them. We might conceivably imagine a God who never punishes or penalizes those who violate his commands or who does not care that his commands are violated. But the point of instituting such a set of commands in the first place would be hard to discern. That a God who institutes commands regarding the behavior of human beings likewise makes provision for the punishment of those who violate his commands appears far likelier.

Thomas Aquinas, by contrast, describes a God who encourages human beings to follow his counsels, where the counsels are designed to benefit those who carry them out. The picture he presents is a picture of a caring God. Thomas speaks of a God who endows human beings with liberty, not just the freedom to disobey, and who counsels them in various ways. The God described by Thomas punishes those who violate his commands, but he also counsels them into avenues of behavior that are in their own best interests.

Augmenting this picture with moral expectation preserves the idea that God is a caring God, encouraging human beings into avenues of behavior that are in their own best interests. But it adds a new element: God forms expectations about human behavior that are not in the form of commands. And human beings are discouraged from the failure to carry them out. Thus, just as God encourages certain behavior that he does not require, other behavior he discourages but does not forbid. And just as God's encouragement of certain behavior reflects a caring concern in the account presented by Thomas, I believe his discouragement of behavior may likewise reflect a caring concern.

Thomas may well be in agreement on this matter. In one passage he distinguishes two types of moral duty (*S.T.*, Ia IIae, 99, Art. 5). When reason dictates that something must be done to ensure the order of virtue, one type of duty arises. When reason informs that something is useful for the order of virtue, a different type of duty arises, one that does not fall under a precept and is not expressed in terms of a command or prohibition. If a failure to carry out a duty of the second type is not prohibited, the violation of such duties may from God's perspective be discouraged but not forbidden. To what extent the class of such duties overlaps with non-obligatory moral expectations, however, is far from clear.

Endowing human beings with liberty to carry out his counsels also makes carrying out God's expectations possible. And if God believes that carrying out his counsels is in the best interests of human beings, we might plausibly suppose that God likewise believes that carrying out his expectations is in the interests of human beings. A God who designs his counsels for the well being of those who carry them out does not appear likely to design his expectations to the detriment of those who carry them out. Perhaps they are not designed to be in the best interests of human beings, but supposing that they are regarded by God as serving some type of good or worthwhile end appears plausible.

If the formation of moral expectations reflects the concern of a caring God, then God is not indifferent to whether the expectations are carried out. If God forms a moral expectation that human beings perform acts of a certain type, then he is not indifferent to whether or not they perform these acts. Since God discourages human beings from failing to carry out these expectations, his reaction to their failure to do so may be one of disappointment. Whereas the failure to carry out the commands of God suffices to evoke reactions of anger or wrath on God's part (and the Old Testament contains many references to this phenomenon), the failure to carry out the expectations of God that are not at the same time requirements is presumably a different matter. Though God might sometimes react with anger at the failure to carry out these expectations, such feelings of anger are no doubt mitigated by the realization that the failure in question violates no moral obligation.

In summary, views which focus exclusively on the commands of God as expressions of his will regarding human beings seem to be unreasonably restrictive. The scholastic distinction between the commands of God and the counsels of God introduces the dimension of human liberty. God's counsels are recommendations human beings are at liberty to follow or to decline from following. Because the counsels of God are designed to benefit those who follow them, the notion of a God who issues such counsels is one of a caring God.

My suggestion has been to augment this picture with the addition of God's moral expectations. If human beings are capable of forming expectations that are non-obligatory, the same is surely true of God. Whereas the addition of God's counsels to the moral picture opens up the possibility of human acts that are recommended but not required, the addition of non-obligatory moral expectation opens up the possibility of human acts that are discouraged but not forbidden. Specifically, the discouraged but not forbidden acts are those are those that constitute the failure to carry out the non-obligatory moral expectations of God.

In what follows I turn to the view that the formation of non-obligatory moral expectations is not part of God's nature. On this view someone might maintain that God's nature precludes the formation of moral expectations directed at human beings that they are not morally required to carry out.

Elsewhere I have discussed the hostile reactions with which the counsels of Thomas Aquinas were greeted by some of the leading figures of the Protestant Reformation (Mellema, 1991, pp. 49–54). The reasons for the hostility, in brief, are these. The practice of selling indulgences in the Holy Roman Catholic Church was based upon the assumption that different saints performed enough good acts so that they completed their lives with a surplus of good over evil. A portion of this accrued treasury of merit could then be purchased and applied to the account of someone facing penalties for having accumulated a surplus of evil over good.

Many people were appalled by this arrangement and the corruption that accompanied it, but the Reformers identified the underlying problem as the notion that human beings are capable of producing a surplus of good over evil. They became convinced that morally good or praiseworthy acts can never be performed apart from moral duty, and hence a treasury of merit is impossible. In particular, a praiseworthy performance of an action by a human being is invariably something commanded by God. No works of supererogation are possible on their view, and they bitterly denounced the scholastic notion of a divine counsel as enabling or accommodating supererogation. In short, the sale of indulgences was made possible because of an underlying theology that drew a distinction between the commands of God and the counsels of God.

Martin Luther and John Calvin believed that God's nature does not allow for the scholastic concept of a counsel. To issue optional recommendations to human beings is not part of God's nature. According to Calvin, "God is entitled to all that we are and have; hence there can be no supererogatory works (Calvin, 1963, p. 781)." And Calvin approvingly quotes St. Augustine as saying, "The saints attribute nothing to their merit (*Ibid.*, p. 789)." No merit is generated by the praiseworthy acts of human beings, even through the acts of the saints. They are merely following the law of God.

Philip Melanchthon, another Reformation writer, joins Luther and Calvin in renouncing the scholastic distinction and shares some of their hostility toward the idea that some of God's laws can be regarded as optional recommendations. At the same time, Melanchthon makes a curious exception for celibacy (Melanchton, 1969, p. 59). On his view, all of God's ordinances are commands with this single exception. He declares that, as far as he knows, celibacy is the only instance of a counsel to be found in the Gospels. God does not command human beings to be celibate; those who marry do not violate God's commands. Nevertheless, God recommends that human beings remain celibate, and their compliance to this recommendation is optional.

Aside from the exception of celibacy in Melanchthon's thought, the Reformation thinkers find the scholastic notion of a counsel abhorrent and incompatible with God's nature. They allow no place for works of supererogation, and the Islamic category of the recommended likewise has no place in their conception of human morality. God does not recommend courses of action to human beings that he does not command.

The Reformers do not speak directly about the possibility of acts which God discourages without forbidding, but I believe that such acts find no place in their conception of morality. Their view of right and wrong appears to be rooted in the ordinances contained in the commands of God. From these ordinances we learn how to conduct our lives as moral agents. And because they are articulated in the form of commands, they are not optional.

Some of these ordinances are in the form of moral obligations to perform certain acts, and some are in the form of moral obligations to refrain from performing various acts. As has already been seen, their conception of morality leaves no room for morally praiseworthy acts that are not morally obligatory. Can there be morally blameworthy acts that are not morally obligatory to omit? Perhaps allowing these acts is logically possible on their views, but allowing these acts does not appear possible from a theological standpoint. On their view, nothing is optional in carrying out what is good or praiseworthy. Performing these acts is obligatory in God's eyes. How then will God allow for what is optional in turning away from that which is morally blameworthy? Given the strength of their convictions about the supremacy of God's commands, the idea that God will not, on their view, regard these acts as obligatory to omit is almost inconceivable.

Calvin refers to human beings as having been bestowed by God with, "The duty that ought in them to be perpetual (*Ibid*. p. 808)." We must appreciate the extent to which Calvin and other figures of the Reformation believed that our moral lives are driven by obedience to duty or obligation that is instituted by God. These duties are made known to human beings by the commands which God issues, and a central part of God's nature on Calvin's view is that God is a being who commands human beings to act in accord with his will. In this passage Calvin is speaking of duty in general. Thus, it refers to the duty to refrain from acting and the duty to act, and I believe it suggests that Calvin's views of the forbidden are as uncompromising as his views of the obligatory.

To think that God will regard morally blameworthy acts by human beings as morally permissible does not seem possible on Calvin's view. On his view God is not likely to regard morally blameworthy behavior as consistent with everything he has commanded. Thus, just as duty contained in the commands of God is powerful enough to swallow up the realm of the praiseworthy, the duty to refrain contained in the commands of God appears powerful enough to swallow up the realm of the blameworthy. Part of God's nature is that his will is manifested through his commands, not through alternative means that allow for that which is optional.

If my interpretation of Calvin is correct, then moral expectation apart from moral obligation is not possible on Calvin's view. Whenever God forms an expectation that a person perform a particular act, then the person has a moral obligation to perform the act. For if the person fails to perform the act, the failure is a blameworthy omission and hence the violation of a duty. And the duty is contained in or entailed by what God has commanded.

Some contemporary theists have been reluctant to acknowledge morally blameworthy but permissible acts. Alan Donagan, for example, takes the position that "demeritorious" or blameworthy acts are either serious enough to constitute the violation of moral obligation, or else they are demeritorious only in a non-moral sense. Self-righteousness and sloth are examples of the former; self-righteous and slothful behavior, on Donagan's view, are morally impermissible. Examples of the latter are ill-breeding, affectation, and coarseness. Engaging in these types of behavior is blameworthy or demeritorious but not morally blameworthy or demeritorious. And for Donagan no middle ground exists (Donagan, 1977, p. 56). Nothing exists which God would regard as morally demeritorious and morally permissible, and hence God's forming moral expectations regarding human beings that are morally non-obligatory is not possible.

In her essay "God's Obligations" Eleonore Stump discusses suberogatory acts and acts of offence, and she basically finds them counter-intuitive, at least as they have been defined in the literature. Her example of an alleged suberogatory act is spreading the story of a colleague's imbecility in a public meeting, and her example of an act of an alleged offence is insisting on the prompt repayment of a loan from someone in financial straits when the lender has no need of the money. She finds examples of this sort counter-intuitive because, "It is hard to understand how an act can be genuinely blameworthy but also permissible (Stump, 1992, p. 480)."

Stump prefers to analyze suberogatory acts and acts of offence as morally obligatory to omit but not required to omit by the rights of any people. Thus, spreading the story of the colleague's imbecility is a violation of moral obligation even though no one has a right to someone's refraining from doing so. And insisting on a timely repayment of the loan is a violation of moral obligation even though no one has a right to someone's omitting to do so. Apparently, then, Stump is in agreement with Donagan in believing that nothing God regards as morally blameworthy is at the same time morally permissible. Everything morally blameworthy ultimately falls off the cliff into the valley of the forbidden.

Neither Donagan nor Stump explicitly appeal to God's nature in reaching their positions, but the end result is that no room exists on their views for God's morally expecting people to perform acts whose performance is non-obligatory. Interestingly, both Donagan and Stump appear to acknowledge acts of supererogation, and on this point they are at variance with the Reformers. Thus, they do not appear to have reason to reject the scholastic distinction between the commands of God and the counsels of God together with the idea that God issues optional recommendations for human beings.

However, on the possibility of morally blameworthy but permissible acts they yield to the supremacy of moral obligation. For Donagan only non-moral blame escapes the obligation to refrain. And for Stump all acts of suberogation and offence are analyzed as morally obligatory to omit, and no morally blameworthy acts are permissible. Thus, for God to form moral expectations that do not carry the force of moral obligation is on their views not possible. All of God's moral expectations regarding the behavior of human beings are in effect commands.

Accordingly, no room can be found in the moral theories of Donagan and Stump for God's discouraging behavior apart from his forbidding this behavior. Their theories allow for God's encouraging human beings to do what is in their best interests, where they are permitted to decline to engage in this behavior. But they allow no room for the mirror-image phenomenon of God's discouraging human beings from doing what is not in their good interests, where they are nevertheless permitted to engage in this detrimental behavior. Human beings who mistakenly believe that morally blameworthy but permissible behavior is possible can on their view believe that God discourages it, but then they are believing that which is not the case.

Earlier we showed that a moral theory which prominently features the commands of God can be enlarged to accommodate human liberty (in a sense richer than the mere ability to disobey) by making room for acts which God encourages but does not require human beings to perform. I then urged the additional enlargement of such a theory to accommodate acts that fulfill God's moral expectations, where not all of these expectations are moral requirements. This additional enlargement captures an additional dimension of human liberty and makes room for acts God discourages but does not forbid.

To the extent that someone agrees with the idea that God values human liberty, the inclusion of God's (non-obligatory) moral expectations appears desirable. Just as human parents find at certain times that encouraging their children to perform good acts which are not strictly required is profitable, we can sensibly imagine the same of God. And just as human parents find at times that discouraging their children from blameworthy behavior which is not strictly forbidden is profitable, we can sensibly imagine the same of God. Parents value their children's ability to make moral choices, and at times they encourage the exercise of this ability in an atmosphere that is not dominated by demands and requirements. The notion that God cares enough about human beings to desire the exercise of the same ability is an attractive one.

Room can be found in the theories of Donagan and Stump for God to discourage blameworthy behavior of a non-moral variety that is optional. (And perhaps room can be found in the theories of Luther and Calvin for God to encourage non-moral praiseworthy behavior that is optional). For Donagan such behavior includes ill-breeding, affectation, and coarseness, and someone accepting Donagan's view is free to argue that God can discourage people from engaging in behavior of these types without regarding this behavior as forbidden. But beyond this rather unremarkable category of acts, their theories do not appear capable of making sense of God's discouraging behavior that does not violate moral duty.

To summarize, the leading figures of the Protestant Reformation were bitterly opposed to the scholastic notion of God's counsels. They maintained that making optional recommendations to human beings is not in the nature of God, that works of supererogation are impossible, and that human beings are incapable of building any type of treasury of merit. They do not specifically address the possibility of acts God discourages without forbidding. But the writings of Calvin, at least, suggest that their opposition to the idea of acts God encourages without requiring is based upon reasons which definitely preclude the possibility of God's considering morally blameworthy acts to be permissible. With the single exception of celibacy in the writings of Melanchthon, the Reformers maintain that God expresses his will in the form of commands. No part of God's nature either recommends meritorious acts that are non-obligatory or discourages demeritorious acts which are not forbidden. In short, God's forming moral expectations of a non-obligatory nature is not possible.

Contemporary theists such as Donagan and Stump do not appear to question the possibility of meritorious, non-obligatory acts. But they reject the possibility of morally blameworthy acts which are permissible, from which we can infer that God does not discourage human beings from performing them. Nor does God form moral expectations concerning the behavior of human beings that do not carry the force of moral obligation.

Eleven

EXPECTATION AND PROFESSIONAL ETHICS

The previous chapters have analyzed the concept of moral expectation in a variety of ways, and the treatment has been largely theoretical. Some stages of the analysis have been accompanied with examples illustrating the issues under discussion, but up to this point no serious effort has been made to explain these issues on a practical level. In this chapter I depart from a style of explanation framed primarily in theoretical terms, and I attempt to provide some insight into how moral expectation operates in people's ordinary experiences on a practical level.

The discussion will attempt to achieve this objective by concentrating upon people's experiences in the context of their work or professional lives. Some moral expectations attach to people as employees or members of organizations, and exploring the types of moral expectations that arise in this context is fruitful. A great deal of work has been produced in business and professional ethics in recent decades, but none of this work deals with moral expectation and the issues surrounding it. An examination of moral expectation in people's professional lives can bring to light important avenues of inquiry which have gone unnoticed by those engaged in business and professional ethics.

This chapter is divided into three parts. The first part examines some moral expectations that attach to individual members of the organization in their roles as employees. The second part highlights three important lessons that can be learned when people make an effort to take these expectations seriously. And the third part contains practical advice as to how people should approach their moral expectations in the workplace. This advice is formulated in terms of assumptions that should not be made about the moral expectations that attach to them in an organizational setting.

The discussion commences, then, with a brief look at some moral expectations that attach to individual employees of an organization. Since great differences exist from one organization to another and since great differences can be found among the job descriptions of the employees within the same organization, not all of the expectations discussed here will apply or attach to all employees. But I believe the expectations discussed here are fairly uniform in their applicability. Most of the items on this list fit the situations of most people who are members of organizations and can appropriately be used to offer them advice or guidance about what is expected of them.

To begin, the individual members or employees of an organization can be expected to familiarize themselves with the goals and policies of the organization and to conduct themselves in accord with them in their professional behavior. Occasionally circumstances may exist in which they are justified in acting contrary to these goals and policies, but within the scope of their professional lives these exceptions are rare.

In addition, the members of an organization can be expected to treat other members with dignity. Just as employees are commonly expected to treat customers and clients with dignity, the same is true of fellow employees. A person of relatively high status within an organization who refuses to acknowledge those of lower status may not be violating a moral obligation, but he or she is likely violating a moral expectation.

The members of an organization can also be expected to practice honesty. This does not mean that we are expected to reveal everything we know about the subject matter at hand. But, generally speaking, we can be expected to refrain from disseminating information we know to be false or misleading. Exaggeration can perhaps be defended in certain circumstances. People often claim that mild forms of exaggeration are frequently taken for granted in certain types of advertising. But not all forms of exaggeration are mild, and we can be expected to refrain from those forms that are destructive in their consequences.

Respect for the privacy of others within an organization is also a moral expectation. We can be expected to refrain from asking our employees to reveal personal information, unless we have a pressing need to do so. We can be expected to refrain from searching an employee's desk, locker, purse, or automobile without permission of the employee or unless we have other justification for doing so (an important document is known to be in an unlocked drawer of the desk of an administrative assistant who is on lunch break). We can be expected to refrain from installing surveillance equipment in lunch areas or restroom facilities to monitor employee conversations. And we can be expected to refrain from spying on an employee, even when we suspect the employee of wrongdoing.

The members of an organization can also be expected to do their best to avoid or eliminate racial or gender stereotypes in their dealings with one another. This will strike some as a point that is so obvious as to hardly need stating. But I believe there are many others who have experienced prejudice or discrimination at the hands of co-workers who will testify to the importance of emphasizing this moral expectation.

Vengeance is likewise something the members of an organization can be expected to avoid. Nothing morally positive can be found about seeking revenge for a real or imagined wrong at the hands of others. Feeling the desire to seek revenge is generally not something that can be controlled by people, but members of an organization can be expected to refrain from actually seeking revenge upon co-workers or upon others connected with the organization.

The items that have been enumerated here are certainly not exhaustive of the moral expectations attaching to the individual members of an organization. I have called attention to some moral expectations representative of the type pertinent to people's professional lives, and clearly many others can be identified. Hopefully the expectations identified here can help us acquire a sense of what can be expected of us regarding our role in an organization.

In some cases one moral expectation might override another moral expectation. For example, the expectation to respect the privacy of a co-worker may be overridden by the expectation to act in accord with the goals and policies of the organization. Suppose that we happen to overhear a co-worker boasting about having stolen merchandise. Under normal circumstances we can be expected to keep the contents of a conversation that is accidentally overheard to ourselves in respect for the other person's right to privacy. But, depending upon the policies of the organization, we might have a contrary expectation to report such conversations to a particular officer within the organization. Thus, we might speak in terms of certain moral expectations as being *prima facie* expectations and others as being all-things-considered expectations.

I turn next to an examination of three lessons that can be learned by those employed in organizations who take seriously the idea that moral expectations attach to them in their professional lives. First, they are able to see that the moral life involves more than carrying out our moral duties and that this insight has important consequences for our decision making in an organizational setting. Second, they are able to appreciate the importance of effectively communicating moral expectations to others in an organizational setting. Third, they are able to discern a difference in the organization's moral climate when members of the organization take seriously their moral expectations in addition to their moral duties.

Several times I have argued that the category of moral expectation is wider than the category of moral duty. Here I urge that an important realization for people in their professional lives is that good ethics involves more than carrying out our moral duties or obligations. When we have successfully carried out our duties, we can easily be convinced that no further effort is necessary. Thus, if we are under no moral obligation to pursue a morally good course of action, we may be tempted to think that inaction on our part is morally justifiable.

Few will question the importance of carrying out the demands of moral duty. Few would question the fact that we must carry out our duties both in our professional lives and in other arenas of life. But many people see no more to the moral life than doing what they are strictly required to do. A realization that the boundaries of moral expectation are wider than the boundaries of moral duty can help people see the confusion in this way of thinking. This realization can help people to see that, just as they are worthy of blame for the failure to do what they are morally required to do, they are also at times worthy of blame for the failure to do what they are morally expected but not required to do.

We are not blameworthy to the same degree on all of the occasions that we incur moral blame through our actions or inaction. Generally speaking, the failure to carry out our moral duty is more serious than the failure to carry out our moral expectations. Thus, other things being equal, we incur greater moral blame for the failure to do what is morally required than the failure to do what is not morally required. However, we can still incur some degree of moral blame for the failure to do what is morally expected of us.

Elsewhere I have argued for the importance of supererogation in people's business and professional lives (Mellema, 1991, pp. 191ff.). The basis for the argument is that, although we can never incur moral blame as the result of failing to perform an act of supererogation, we can incur moral blame for multiple failures to perform an act of supererogation. Repeatedly passing up the opportunity to perform an act of supererogation can be morally blameworthy, depending upon the circumstances, even though omitting a single act of supererogation is never morally blameworthy. For this reason, someone who is serious about the moral life cannot routinely ignore opportunities to perform acts of supererogation. And here moral expectation becomes relevant to supererogation: although people can never be morally expected to perform an act of supererogation, they can be morally expected to perform acts of supererogation on at least an occasional basis.

In their professional lives, then, people cannot afford to ignore opportunities to perform acts of supererogation. But as important as this point is, taking moral expectation seriously in our professional lives is even more important. For whenever we fail to do what we are morally expected to do, our failure is morally blameworthy. Moral blame attaches to the failure to perform acts of supererogation only in a wholesale fashion, but moral blame attaches to each individual failure to do what we are morally expected to do. Because of this, people have a more compelling reason to take stock of their moral expectations. In their professional lives they should not always pass up opportunities to perform acts of supererogation. But carrying out their moral expectations is a matter of even greater concern.

A second lesson those who are members of organizations can learn is the importance of communicating expectations effectively. Children learn what is morally expected of them by adults with whom they are in contact. Through a process of moral maturity they then develop the ability to identify moral expectations largely without the assistance of others. Nevertheless, throughout their adult lives receiving advice from others can be helpful, and this includes their experiences in organizational settings. Sometimes people with a fair amount of ethical sensitivity in other parts of their lives need assistance to discern the moral expectations that attach to them in the workplace.

A person's employer or supervisor can play a pivotal role in this process. Those in positions of leadership can provide valuable assistance to members of the organization by enabling them to discern what is morally expected of them in their roles within the setting of the organization. By communicating moral expectations to those over whom we have supervision, we make possible a heightened sense of moral sensitivity within the organization as a whole. Those in a position of leadership can function as positive role models in the organization by taking their own moral expectations seriously. But if they are able to provide their employees with a clear sense of the moral expectations operative in the organization, their employees are able to do the same.

The effectiveness of people's learning their moral expectations in an organizational setting is dependent upon effective communication. If someone's employer or supervisor comes across as self-righteous in offering advice, the advice may be poorly received. The advice should be conveyed in a manner that is clear, tactful, and diplomatic. Those who have risen to roles of leadership in an organization are likely to have acquired communication skills that will help ensure the effectiveness of this process.

The task of helping others to discern their moral expectations in the workplace need not be confined to those in roles of leadership. At all levels of an organization may be people who are gifted in the type of ethical sensitivity and intuition which may enable them to offer helpful advice to their co-workers. We should not automatically prefer the moral advice that comes from people who happen to occupy lofty positions within the organization. Frequently the advice of a co-worker with whom we have established a relationship of friendship or special rapport can be particularly helpful in extending or deepening our moral awareness or insight. Bird and Waters describe these exchanges as follows:

> Through verbal exchanges people identify, evoke, and establish normative expectations as compelling cultural realities. Moral expressions are articulated to persuade others, to reinforce personal convictions, to criticize, and to justify decisions. Moral expressions are also invoked to praise and to blame, to evaluate and to rationalize. Moral discourse plays a lively role communicating normative expectations, seeking cooperation of others, and rendering judgments (Bird and Waters, 1989. p. 74).

When people in an organization effectively learn how they are expected to conduct themselves in the workplace, a heightened sense of moral awareness across the organization itself begins to take place. And this leads to the third lesson that can be learned by those who participate in the process: the moral climate of the organization is affected. When moral expectation is acknowledged as having a presence in the workplace and when members of the organization make an effort to identify and carry out the moral expectations that attach to them, then an improvement in the moral climate of the workplace is likely to result.

Many people can attest to having worked for organizations whose moral climates are less than desirable. Sometimes organizations seem to breed a spirit of cynicism regarding questions of right and wrong; in more extreme cases a spirit of mockery for good ethics may pervade the moral atmosphere of an organization. The moral climate of an organization can be improved in many different ways, but I believe one of the most effective is by working to implement the process described above. When moral expectations are communicated effectively to the members of the organization so that a widespread sense of people's moral expectations begins to take place, an improvement in the moral climate of the organization is almost certain to result.

In some organizations people are mindful of the goals and policies of the organization, they are mindful of their moral duties, and they are conscientious about conducting themselves accordingly in the workplace. The moral climate in organizations of this type may appear quite desirable, and those employed in such organizations may consider themselves fortunate to be part of an organization with a moral climate that may strike them as enviable.

But when people learn that they are morally expected to pursue courses of action which are not strictly required of them, the possibility of improvement is introduced. When people learn to look beyond what is strictly required of them to discover that they can at times be expected to benefit others within the organization, then the possibility of a moral climate even more desirable becomes evident. When the members of an organization begin to recognize the expectations that morality places upon them and when they begin to resolve to honor these expectations, a new type of atmosphere is created within the organization.

Achieving this type of atmosphere will involve the members of the organization cultivating an awareness of the needs or interests of others within the organization. When people learn to look beyond the strict requirements of morality, they find ways that they can benefit others. The moral expectations that attach to people are usually directed to ways in which they can benefit others or help prevent harm from befalling others. In addition, achieving this type of atmosphere will involve the members of the organization cultivating an awareness of the best interests of the organization. Sometimes we can be expected to perform actions that prevent harm to the organization. If someone is publicly spreading false rumors about the quality of health care at a hospital where a person is employed, the person may not have a moral obligation to step forward and challenge these false allegations. But in all probability he or she can be morally expected to do so.

To summarize, when the members of an organization recognize moral expectation and when they make an effort to carry out these expectations in the workplace, then they are in a position to learn some significant lessons by acquiring insights in three important areas. First, they can acquire insights about the importance of doing more than what is strictly required by duty. Second, they can acquire insights regarding the importance of communicating expectations effectively and the benefits which individual members of the organization can realize when this happens. Third, they can acquire insights into how this process can improve the moral climate of the organization.

Next I turn to some practical advice about how individual members of the organization should regard or approach moral expectation in the workplace.

This advice is formulated in terms of assumptions people should not make about moral expectation in an organizational setting. Altogether there are five assumptions they should resist in their professional lives.

First, people who are employed in organizations should not assume that they are excused from being concerned about moral expectation if their role in the organization is insignificant, if they occupy an inferior or subordinate position in the institutional hierarchy, or if they are in a position of performing menial tasks. They should not lose sight of their importance and dignity as moral agents and of their potential for being of service to others in the organization. Sometimes people have a tendency to assume that those who are in the capacity of making decisions are the only people who need to be concerned about the moral dimension of the workplace. Obviously this assumption is fallacious. From the foregoing discussion we can infer that people having moral expectations are not confined to those in positions of leadership, for otherwise those in positions of leadership would have no need to communicate moral expectations to those whom they supervise.

Second, members of organizations should not assume that the sheer size of the organization diminishes the moral importance of our carrying out our expectations. In Chapter Seven I urge rejection of the view that someone's share of moral responsibility for what happens diminishes as the number of people sharing responsibility for the same state of affairs increases. Just because the number of people sharing responsibility for the same state of affairs increases, we cannot deduce that each person's responsibility for it is diluted or diminished. Moral responsibility is not like a pie, where only so much is available to go around and where the size of one's slice grows smaller as the responsibility is shared with more and more people.

A parallel point applies here. When the people making up an organization have some moral expectations in common, they should not assume that the significance of each member's carrying out his or her expectation is lessened or diminished as the result of being shared with many others in the organization. For example, if each member is expected to act in accord with the goals and policies of the organization, an individual member of a large organization may be tempted to assume that the importance of carrying out this expectation on his or her part is very insignificant.

Other members of the organization may perform acts that affect the practical importance or urgency of one member's carrying out a moral expectation. Suppose that Howard is one of many switchboard operators working for a medium-sized corporation. On weekends only two operators are on duty, and they are expected to allow no calls to go unanswered. One Saturday through a mix-up in scheduling Howard finds himself the only operator on duty. A co-worker is called at home and graciously agrees to come in on her day off so that two operators are on duty. We might argue that the co-worker's coming to work takes a great deal of pressure off Howard and diminishes the practical importance of his carrying out the expectations which attach to him. He is no longer expected to answer every incoming call, and if he takes off for a few minutes of relaxation the telephones are still covered.

Nevertheless, Howard should not consider his expectations less important from a moral point of view. The co-worker's arrival may in the sense indicated diminish the practical importance of Howard's fulfilling his expectations, but to conclude that her arrival diminishes the moral importance of his doing so is fallacious. For suppose that both of them begin to watch the television in the employee lounge during a very slack period and as a result an incoming call goes unanswered. Both are blameworthy for the unanswered call, and we will be hard pressed to see how the degree of moral blame borne by Howard is any less owing to the mere fact that it is shared with another operator.

Third, members of organizations should not assume that everything they ought to know about what is expected of them in the workplace will be pointed out to them. Hopefully their employer or supervisor will communicate to them the essential facts about what they are expected to do and what they expected to refrain from doing in carrying out their job assignment. And hopefully co-workers will lend assistance in this process as well. But part of what is involved in being a responsible employee is taking the initiative to learn what is expected of him or her on the job. We might even say that members of an organization have a meta-expectation to learn about the expectations that attach to someone in the capacity of being an employee of the organization.

Fourth, those who are employed by organizations should not assume that the expectations attaching to a person in the workplace remain invariant over time. Expectations that attached to us in the past may no longer do so in the future, and we may come to take on new expectations over time. Some of the reasons for changes in the expectations which attach to us are somewhat obvious: a person has a new job assignment, the person has a new supervisor with different ideas about employee expectations, or the organization itself is acquired by a new owner or parent company.

But subtler reasons for changes in the expectations attaching to members of organizations are possible. Earlier reference was made to the possibility of changes in the moral climate of the organization. If improvements are made in the moral climate of a firm, then changes in the expectations that attach to the firm's employees will doubtless occur. For example, the employees of a prominent firm may have routinely amused themselves with off-color stories and jokes while on the job. With changes in the moral climate of the firm, such stories and jokes may no longer be considered acceptable, and the expectation to refrain from telling them may come to attach to all employees.

Fifth, members of organizations should not assume that everyone else will approach their expectations in a uniform fashion. Some of a person's co-workers might be conscientious about identifying the expectations that attach to them and diligent about carrying them out. Other co-workers might display no interest whatever in identifying the expectations which attach to them and little or no interest in carrying them out.

Where little moral guidance comes from those in a position of leadership, differences are likely to be wider than if more guidance is provided. For when supervisory personnel begin to articulate and identify the moral expectations that attach to their employees, then, as has already been seen, a heightened sense of moral awareness is likely to develop among the employees to whom this advice is communicated. And this, in turn, leads to a greater uniformity in the way that these employees think about and carry out their moral expectations.

In this book I have attempted to call attention to a dimension of the moral life that has received relatively little attention. The concept of moral expectation frequently surfaces in ordinary conversation, people clearly make an effort to include it as a component of moral education, and it is frequently referred to by professional ethicists. But people seldom if ever attempt to analyze it or examine it in relation to other moral concepts.

This discussion of moral expectation has been intended as an introductory survey. The topics comprising the individual chapters have been selected in the hopes of presenting a picture of moral expectation which is well rounded and which is more or less accessible to those with limited training in ethics. But obviously much more can be said about each of these topics and about moral expectation in general. My intent has not been to probe these issues in the depth to which some might be accustomed in scholarly treatments of ethical issues. Nor have I attempted to comment on every possible connection between the concept of moral expectation and other moral concepts.

What has been said about moral expectation presupposes that readers are familiar with the notion from ordinary conversation. When a child is told by a parent that he or she is expected to perform a particular task before being allowed outdoors, the child presumably understands what is meant and anyone hearing the conversation presumably understands what is meant. To the extent that the account of moral expectation presented here reflects this notion from ordinary discourse, I believe my project is capable of illuminating and clarifying a familiar concept to those who are already acquainted with it. To the extent that this account casts a familiar concept in a way that is artificial and out of keeping with the way ordinary people think about this concept, it will doubtless be of little benefit. For this reason I have resisted a treatment in which every component of the discussion is oriented to elaborate definitions of key concepts in terms which may not be faithful to ordinary usage.

Essential to this treatment of moral expectation is the insistence that it is not the same as moral obligation and that it is not always a moral requirement to carry out our moral expectations. Contemporary moral philosophy has been preoccupied with discussions concerning moral duty, responsibility, and rights, and these discussions are essentially about moral requirements (since rights involve moral requirements on the part of others who must respect these rights).

Thus, to say that contemporary moral philosophy has been largely preoccupied with the requirements of morality is not an exaggeration, and this is true of those aligned with the both Kantian and consequentialist traditions of morality.

To say that work dealing with the requirements of morality holds a position of dominance is not to say that all recent work in ethics follows this path. Recent work in virtue ethics has followed a different path, and we have every reason to be enthusiastic about this development. Emergent signs of interest can be found regarding moral concepts less forceful than what is obligatory and what is forbidden. In Chapter Four attention was focussed on the work of several philosophers who believe in a sense of the term "ought" weaker than moral obligation. On the basis of the discussion in Chapter Four the kinship between this weaker sense of ought and the concept of moral expectation is clear.

Nevertheless, philosophers have shown a reluctance to acknowledge the legitimacy of moral concepts that fall short of being moral requirements. Opposition to the notion of supererogation can be traced as far back as the writings of the Protestant Reformation, as has been seen in Chapter Ten. Many feel a powerful urge to judge that anything morally praiseworthy falls under the scope of moral obligation. Thus, a moral agent with an opportunity to perform a morally praiseworthy act has a moral obligation to perform the act, and hence the failure to perform the act is morally forbidden. On this view, we are morally required to perform every praiseworthy act we have an opportunity to perform.

Those who oppose the possibility of supererogation are not committed to opposing the possibility of non-obligatory moral expectation. For someone can hold that every morally praiseworthy act falls under the scope of moral obligation without holding that every morally blameworthy act falls under the scope of the morally forbidden. And if some morally blameworthy acts are permissible, then the possibility of non-obligatory moral expectation is opened up. If the omission of a non-obligatory moral expectation is possible, then presumably non-obligatory moral expectation itself is possible.

However, if a person is genuinely committed to the position that every morally praiseworthy act falls under the scope of moral obligation, the person will not likely acknowledge the possibility of morally blameworthy but permissible acts. If a person views moral obligation as so pervasive that it swallows up every act that is morally praiseworthy, the person's viewing the moral obligation to refrain as failing to swallow up all acts that are morally blameworthy is unlikely. To put things another way, if a person's view of moral obligation is so strict and demanding that morally praiseworthy acts are never permissible to omit, the person's believing that morally blameworthy acts are sometimes permissible to perform would be surprising. If moral obligation is so demanding that morally praiseworthy acts are invariably obligatory, the demands of moral obligation do not allow for the performance of morally blameworthy acts.

One message conveyed in this book is that morality is not as strict and demanding as some have alleged. The opening example in Chapter One sets the tone of the subsequent discussion by depicting a situation in which opening the door for a total stranger is morally expected of someone and the failure to carry out the expectation is morally blameworthy without constituting the violation of duty. Such a failure might be blameworthy to a degree that is minimal, but it is blameworthy nevertheless. In a strict and demanding system of morality someone would be forced either to judge that he or she has a moral obligation to open the door or to deny that anything is morally blameworthy in failing to open the door.

But surely obligation is not a plausible category to assign to the failure of common courtesy directed at a total stranger. That one is duty-bound to practice it whenever the opportunity arises does not seem to be in the nature of common courtesy, just as (in David Little's example) gift giving is not by its nature something we are duty-bound to carry out. On the other hand, judging that nothing is the least bit blameworthy in failing to open the door for the person whose arms are laden with packages struggling to come in from the rain appears likewise counter-intuitive. Surely something is wrong with standing there watching the person struggle and doing absolutely nothing. I believe the account of moral expectation developed in the preceding chapters strikes just the right balance in cases of this type. When someone is expected to act in a courteous manner to another, the failure to do so is blameworthy but need not be forbidden.

In Chapters Nine and Ten reference is made in several places to Islamic codes of ethics which divide moral acts into the categories of the required, the forbidden, the recommended, the discouraged, and the permitted. The category of the recommended corresponds roughly to the category of supererogation, according to Julia Driver, while the category of the discouraged corresponds roughly to the category of the suberogatory. I have urged, in addition, that the failure of non-obligatory moral expectation falls into the category of the discouraged. Thus, while we are never forbidden to fail to carry out our non-obligatory moral expectations, we are discouraged from doing so.

Clearly Islamic codes of ethics containing these categories do not subscribe to a strict and demanding view of moral obligation. In this way they appear capable of accommodating what people say about moral expectation in ordinary discourse. They also appear to be more in touch with the way people think about morality than contemporary writers who seem preoccupied with the requirements of morality.

Acknowledging the insights found in the moral systems of other cultures and traditions can be of great value. In particular, we may plausibly acknowledge the categories of the recommended and the discouraged. I believe that these categories are reflected in the way people talk and think about the moral life. Sometimes we recommend that others perform actions of various sorts without thinking that they are in any way required to perform these actions. And sometimes we discourage people from performing actions of various types without thinking that they are required to refrain from these actions. As has been seen, moral expectation is, roughly speaking, the flip side of moral discouragement. People who are expected to perform an act can rightly be discouraged from omitting to perform the act, and people who are expected to omit an act can rightly be discouraged from performing it.

I have suggested that moral expectation is a concept familiar to ordinary people. Most people are aware that certain actions people can be expected to perform and certain actions people can be expected to refrain from performing. People recognize that some type of negative moral status is attached to the failure to carry out a moral expectation, and people recognize that moral education consists, in part, in learning what is morally expected of a person. In the foregoing chapters I hope to have shed some light on this important but neglected dimension of the moral life.

WORKS CITED

Appiah, Anthony. (1986). "Racism and Moral Pollution," *The Philosophical Forum*, 18, pp. 185–202.

Archard, David. (1986). "Moral Partiality" *Midwest Studies in Philosophy, Volume XX*, eds., Peter French, Theodore E. Ueling, Jr., and Howard K. Wettstein. Notre Dame, Indiana: Notre Dame University Press, pp. 129–141.

Arthur, John. (1993). "World Hunger and Moral Obligation: The Case Against Singer," in *Vice and Virtue in Everyday Life*, eds. C. Sommers and F. Sommers. New York: Harcourt Brace Publishing Co., pp. 845–852.

Audi, Robert. (1997). *Moral Knowledge and Ethical Character*. New York: Oxford University Press.

Baier, Annette. (1986). "Trust and Antitrust," *Ethics*, pp. 231–260.

Barber, Bernard. (1983). *The Logic and Limits of Trust*. New Brunswick, New Jersey: Rutgers University Press.

Bird, Frederick and Waters, James. (1989). "The Moral Muteness of Managers,"*California Management Review*, 32, pp. 73–88.

Blum, Laurence. (1980). *Friendship, Altruism, and Morality*. London: Routledge and Kegan Paul.

Calvin, John. (1963). *Institutes of the Christian Religion*, eds., John T. McNeill and Ford Lewis Battles. Philadelphia: Westminster Press.

Card, Claudia. (1972). "On Mercy," Philosophical Review, 81, pp. 182–207.

Chisholm, Roderick. (1963). "Supererogation and Offence: A Conceptual Scheme for Ethics," *Ratio*, 5, pp. 1–14.

Chisholm, Roderick and Sosa, Ernest. (1966). "Intrinsic Preferability and the Problem of Supererogation," *Synthese*, 16, pp. 321–331.

Coleman, Jules. (2001). "The Conventionality Thesis," *Social, Political and Legal Philosophy*, eds., Ernest Sosa and Enrique Villanueva. Boston: Blackwell Publishing Co., pp. 354–387.

Cullity, Garrett. (1997). "Practical Theory," *Ethics and Practical Reason*, eds., Garrett Cullity and Berys Gaut. New York: Oxford University Press, pp. 101–124.

Donagan, Alan. (1997). *The Theory of Morality*. Chicago: University of Chicago Press.

Driver, Julia. (1992). "The Suberogatory," *Australasian Journal of Philosophy*, 70, pp. 286–293.

Fishkin, James. (1982). *The Limits of Obligation*. New Haven: Yale University Press.

Frey, R. G.(1974). "On Causal Consequences," *Canadian Journal of Philosophy*, 4, pp. 365–379.

Irwin, T. H. (1997). "Practical Reason Divided: Aquinas and His Critics," *Ethics and Practical Reason*, eds., Garrett Cullity and Berys Gaut. New York: Oxford University Press, pp. 189–214.

Kutz, Christopher. (2001). "The Judicial Community," *Social, Political and Legal Philosophy*, eds., Ernest Sosa and Enrique Villanueva. Boston: Blackwell Publishing Co., pp. 442–469.

Little, David. (1992). "The Law of Supererogation," *The Love Commandments*, eds., Edmund N. Santurri and William Werehowski. Washington D.C.: Georgetown University Press, pp. 157–181.

Lyons, David. (1965). *The Forms and Limits of Utilitarianism*. London: Oxford University Press.

_____. (1984). *Ethics and the Rule of Law*. Cambridge, England: Cambridge University Press.

Mackie, J. L (1977). *Ethics: Inventing Right and Wrong*. London: Penguin Books.

Melanchthon, Philip. (1969). *Loci Communes Theologici*, ed. Wilhelm Pauck. Philadelphia: Westminster Press.

Mellema, Gregory. (1991). *Beyond the Call of Duty*. Albany: State University of New York Press.

_____. (1997). *Collective Responsibility*. Amsterdam and Atlanta: Editions Rodopi, B.V.

_____. (1998). "Moral Expectation," *The Journal of Value Inquiry*, 32, pp. 479–488.

Mill, John Stuart. (1971) *Utilitarianism*, ed., Samuel Gorovitz. New York: Bobbs-Merrill Publishing Co.

Miller, Seumas. (2001). *Social Action*. Cambridge, England: Cambridge University Press.

Nozick, Robert. (1974) *Anarchy, State and Utopia*. Cambridge, Mass.: Harvard University Press.

_____. (1993). *The Nature of Rationality*. Princeton: Princeton University Press.

Parfit, Derek. (1984). *Reasons and Persons*. Oxford: Clarendon Press.

Rickless, Samuel. (1997). "The Doctrine of Doing and Allowing," *Philosophical Review*, 106, pp. 555–575.

Ricoeur, Paul. (1967). *The Symbolism of Evil*. New York: Harper and Row Publishing Co.

Seligman, Adam. (1997). *The Problem of Trust*. Princeton: Princeton University Press.

Shapiro, Scott. (2001). "Judicial Can't," *Social, Political and Legal Philosophy*, eds., Ernest Sosa and Enrique Villanueva. Boston: Blackwell Publishing Co., pp. 530–557.

Sidgwick, Henry. (1981). *The Methods of Ethics*. Indianapolis: Hackett Publishing Co.

Simmons, A. John. (1981). 'Reasonable Expectations and Obligations," *Southern Journal of Philosophy*, 19, pp. 123–127.

Smiley, Marion. (1996). "Battered Women and Bombed-Out Cities: A Question of Responsibility," *Midwest Studies in Philosophy, Volume XX*, eds., Peter French, Theodore E. Ueling, Jr., and Howard K. Wettstein. Notre Dame, Indiana: Notre Dame University Press, pp. 15–35.

Stump, Eleonore. (1992). "God's Obligations," *Philosophical Perspectives*, 6, ed., James Tomberlin. Atascadero, CA: Ridgeview Publishing, pp. 475–491.

Thomson, Judith Jarvis. (1971). "A Defense of Abortion," *Philosophy and Public Affairs*, 1, pp. 47–66.

Whelan, John. (1991). "Famine and Charity," *Southern Journal of Philosophy*, 29, pp. 149–166.

Widerker, David. (1991). "Frankfurt on 'Ought Implies Can' and Alternative Possibilities," *Analysis,* 51, pp. 222–224.

Widerker, David and Katzoff, Charlotte. (1994). "Zimmerman on Moral Responsibility," *Analysis,* 54, pp. 285–287.

Williams, Bernard. (1985). *Ethics and the Limits of Philosophy.* Cambridge, Mass.: Harvard University Press.

Wittgenstein, Ludwig. (1965). *The Blue and Brown Books.* New York: Harper and Row.

Wolf, Susan. (1992). "Morality and Partiality," *Philosophical Perspectives,* 6, ed., James Tomberlin. Atascadero, CA: Ridgeview Publishing, pp. 243–259.

Zimmerman, Michael. (1985). "Sharing Responsibility,"*American Philosophical Quarterly*, 22, pp. 115–122.

———. (1993). "Obligation, Responsibility, and Alternate Possibilities," *Analysis*, 53, pp. 51–53.

———. (1997). "A Plea for Accuses," *American Philosophical Quarterly*, 34, pp. 229–243.

ABOUT THE AUTHOR

Gregory Mellema is Professor of Philosophy at Calvin College, where he has taught from 1975 to 1976 and from 1978 to the present.

Mellema received his doctorate from the University of Massachusetts at Amherst in 1974. He was an instructor at St. Olaf College from 1974 to 1975. He later earned a Masters Degree in Business Administration from the University of Michigan, a degree which qualified him to teach and write about business ethics. He has frequently taught courses on this and related topics at Aquinas College as well as Calvin College.

He is the author of three other books, *Individuals, Groups, and Shared Moral Responsibility*, *Beyond the Call of Duty*, and *Collective Responsibility*, and of a booklet, *The Bottom Line*. He has contributed articles to five reference works, *Magill's Reference in Ethics*, *The Oxford Companion to Philosophy*, *Encyclopedia of Contemporary Ethical Issues*, *Encyclopedia of Applied Ethics*, and *Encyclopedia of Ethical Issues in Politics and the Media*.

His articles have appeared in over twenty different journals, including *American Philosophical Quarterly*, *Canadian Journal of Philosophy*, *Philosophical Studies*, *Australasian Journal of Philosophy*, *Philosophia*, and *Analysis*. Most of his recent articles deal with issues in ethics, both theoretical and applied, but he has also published in the areas of philosophy of language, logic, and the philosophy of education.

INDEX

VIBS

The **Value Inquiry Book Series** is co-sponsored by:

Titles Published

1. Noel Balzer, *The Human Being as a Logical Thinker*

2. Archie J. Bahm, *Axiology: The Science of Values*

3. H. P. P. (Hennie) Lötter, *Justice for an Unjust Society*

4. H. G. Callaway, *Context for Meaning and Analysis: A Critical Study in the Philosophy of Language*

5. Benjamin S. Llamzon, *A Humane Case for Moral Intuition*

6. James R. Watson, *Between Auschwitz and Tradition: Postmodern Reflections on the Task of Thinking.* A volume in **Holocaust and Genocide Studies**

7. Robert S. Hartman, *Freedom to Live: The Robert Hartman Story*, Edited by Arthur R. Ellis. A volume in **Hartman Institute Axiology Studies**

8. Archie J. Bahm, *Ethics: The Science of Oughtness*

9. George David Miller, *An Idiosyncratic Ethics; Or, the Lauramachean Ethics*

10. Joseph P. DeMarco, *A Coherence Theory in Ethics*

11. Frank G. Forrest, *Valuemetrics^{x}: The Science of Personal and Professional Ethics.* A volume in **Hartman Institute Axiology Studies**

12. William Gerber, *The Meaning of Life: Insights of the World's Great Thinkers*

13. Richard T. Hull, Editor, *A Quarter Century of Value Inquiry: Presidential Addresses of the American Society for Value Inquiry.* A volume in **Histories and Addresses of Philosophical Societies**

14. William Gerber, *Nuggets of Wisdom from Great Jewish Thinkers: From Biblical Times to the Present*

15. Sidney Axinn, *The Logic of Hope: Extensions of Kant's View of Religion*

75. Warren E. Steinkraus, *Taking Religious Claims Seriously: A Philosophy of Religion*, Edited by Michael H. Mitias. A volume in **Universal Justice**

76. Thomas Magnell, Editor, *Values and Education*

77. Kenneth A. Bryson, *Persons and Immortality*. A volume in **Natural Law Studies**

78. Steven V. Hicks, *International Law and the Possibility of a Just World Order: An Essay on Hegel's Universalism*. A volume in **Universal Justice**

79. E. F. Kaelin, *Texts on Texts and Textuality: A Phenomenology of Literary Art*, Edited by Ellen J. Burns

80. Amihud Gilead, *Saving Possibilities: A Study in Philosophical Psychology*. A volume in Philosophy and Psychology

81. André Mineau, *The Making of the Holocaust: Ideology and Ethics in the Systems Perspective*. A volume in **Holocaust and Genocide Studies**

82. Howard P. Kainz, *Politically Incorrect Dialogues: Topics Not Discussed in Polite Circles*

83. Veikko Launis, Juhani Pietarinen, and Juha Räikkä, Editors, *Genes and Morality: New Essays*. A volume in **Nordic Value Studies**

84. Steven Schroeder, *The Metaphysics of Cooperation: A Study of F. D. Maurice*

85. Caroline Joan ("Kay") S. Picart, *Thomas Mann and Friedrich Nietzsche: Eroticism, Death, Music, and Laughter*. A volume in **Central-European Value Studies**

86. G. John M. Abbarno, Editor, *The Ethics of Homelessness: Philosophical Perspectives*

87. James Giles, Editor, *French Existentialism: Consciousness, Ethics, and Relations with Others*. A volume in **Nordic Value Studies**

88. Deane Curtin and Robert Litke, Editors, *Institutional Violence*. A volume in **Philosophy of Peace**

117.   Robert T. Radford, *Cicero: A Study in the Origins of Republican Philosophy*. A volume in **Studies in the History of Western Philosophy**

118.   Arleen L. F. Salles and María Julia Bertomeu, Editors, *Bioethics: Latin American Perspectives*. A volume in **Philosophy in Latin America**

119.   Nicola Abbagnano, *The Human Project: The Year 2000*, with an Interview by Guiseppe Grieco. Translated from Italian by Bruno Martini and Nino Langiulli. Edited with an introduction by Nino Langiulli. A volume in **Studies in the History of Western Philosophy**

120.   Daniel M. Haybron, Editor, *Earth's Abominations: Philosophical Studies of Evil*. A volume in **Personalist Studies**

121.   Anna T. Challenger, *Philosophy and Art in Gurdjieff's* Beelzebub*: A Modern Sufi Odyssey*

122.   George David Miller, *Peace, Value, and Wisdom: The Educational Philosophy of Daisaku Ikeda*. A volume in **Daisaku Ikeda Studies**

123.   Haim Gordon and Rivca Gordon, *Sophistry and Twentieth-Century Art*

124.   Thomas O. Buford and Harold H. Oliver, Editors *Personalism Revisited: Its Proponents and Critics*. A volume in **Histories and Addresses of Philosophical Societies**

125.   Avi Sagi, *Albert Camus and the Philosophy of the Absurd*. Translated from Hebrew by Batya Stein

126.   Robert S. Hartman, *The Knowledge of Good: Critique of Axiological Reason*. Expanded translation from the Spanish by Robert S. Hartman. Edited by Arthur R. Ellis and Rem B. Edwards.A volume in **Hartman Institute Axiology Studies**

127.   Alison Bailey and Paula J. Smithka, Editors. *Community, Diversity, and Difference: Implications for Peace.* A volume in **Philosophy of Peace**

128.   Oscar Vilarroya, *The Dissolution of Mind: A Fable of How Experience Gives Rise to Cognition*. A volume in **Cognitive Science**

129.   Paul Custodio Bube and Jeffery Geller, Editors, *Conversations with Pragmatism: A Multi-Disciplinary Study*. A volume in **Studies in Pragmatism and Values**